Da...

Reunion, Dark...
The Woo...

Reunion shows the meeting betw... ...er nearly twenty years of separation: 'It would be hard to over-praise the way Mr Mamet suggests behind the probing, joshing family chat an extraordinary sense of pain and loss . . . although the play has a strong social comment about the destructively cyclical effect of divorce, it is neither sour nor defeatist.' *Guardian*

Dark Pony: 'A subtle, lyrical, dreamlike vignette . . . In it, a father tells his five-year-old daughter a story about an Indian boy and his pony . . . It's a lovely little tale about childhood memories and emotions.' *Star Tribune*

A Life in the Theatre portrays the relationship between an older and younger actor, onstage and backstage: 'As so often in Mamet, a sense of desolation lies behind the laughter. In the spare, beautifully poised dialogue of the off-stage scenes he captures all the tension and rivalry between the old stager and the young pretender, scrupulously charting the balance of power as it shifts from age to youth . . . Mamet brings us to the heart of transience and loss.' *Sunday Telegraph*

In *The Woods* a young man and woman spend the night in a cabin in the woods: 'a beautifully conceived love story.' *Chicago Daily News*

In *Lakeboat* eight crew members of a merchant ship exchange wild fantasies about sex, gambling and violence: 'Richly overheard talk . . . loopy, funny construction.' *Village Voice*

Edmond: 'A stunning amorality play, glittering and disturbing, suspended in the dark void of contemporary New York. It is also a technically adventurous piece pared brilliantly to the bone, highly theatrical in its scenic elisions.' *Financial Times*

David Mamet was born in Chicago in 1947. He studied at Goddard College, Vermont (where he was later Artist-in-Residence), and at the Neighborhood Playhouse School of Theater in New York. His first and many subsequent plays were first performed by the St Nicholas Theater Company, Chicago, of which he was a founding member and Artistic Director. In 1978 he became Associate Artistic Director of the Goodman Theater, Chicago, where *American Buffalo* had been first staged in 1975, subsequently winning the Obie Award and opening on Broadway in 1977 and at the National Theatre, London in 1978. *Sexual Perversity in Chicago* and *Duck Variations* (Regent Theatre, 1977), *A Life in the Theatre* (Open Space, 1979), *Glengarry Glen Ross* (National Theatre, 1983; Pulitzer Prize for Drama 1984), *Edmond* (Royal Court, 1985), *Oleanna* (Royal Court and Duke of York's Theatre, 1993) and *The Cryptogram* (Ambassadors Theatre, 1994) have also been staged in London. Other plays include *Reunion*, *The Woods*, *The Water Engine* (all first staged in 1977), *Lakeboat* (1982) and *The Disappearance of the Jews* (1983). For the cinema he wrote the screenplays for *The Postman Always Rings Twice*, *The Verdict*, *House of Games*, *The Untouchables*, *Things Change* (written with Shel Silverstein), *Glengarry Glen Ross*, *We're No Angels*, *Hoffa*, *The Deer Slayer*, *High and Low* and *Ace in the Hole*.

DAVID MAMET

Plays: 2

Reunion
Dark Pony
A Life in the Theatre
The Woods
Lakeboat
Edmond

Methuen Drama

METHUEN CONTEMPORARY DRAMATISTS

This collection first published in Great Britain in 1996
by Methuen Drama

Random House UK Limited
20 Vauxhall Bridge Road, London SW1V 2SA
and Australia, New Zealand and South Africa

Random House UK Limited Reg. No. 954009

3 5 7 9 10 8 6 4 2

Reunion was first published in Great Britain in 1996 by Methuen Drama,
copyright © 1979, 1996 by David Mamet
Dark Pony was first published in Great Britain in 1996 by Methuen Drama,
copyright © 1979, 1996 by David Mamet
A Life in the Theatre was first published in Great Britain in 1996 by Methuen
Drama, copyright © 1977, 1989, 1996 by David Mamet
The Woods was first published in Great Britain in 1996 by Methuen Drama,
copyright © 1979, 1996 by David Mamet
Lakeboat was first published in Great Britain in 1996 by Methuen Drama,
copyright © 1981, 1996 by David Mamet
Edmond was first published in Great Britain in 1996 by Methuen London,
copyright © 1983, 1986, 1996 by David Mamet
This collection © 1996 by Methuen Drama

The author has asserted his moral rights

ISBN 0-413-68740-6

A CIP catalogue record for this book is available from the British Library

Typeset by Wilmaset, Birkenhead, Wirral
Printed and bound in Great Britain by Cox & Wyman Ltd, Reading, Berkshire

Caution

Contents

David Mamet:
A Chronology

PLAYS	USA	UK
Duck Variations, St Nicholas Theater Company, Chicago, 1972; Regent Theatre, London, 1977	1972	1977
Sexual Perversity in Chicago, Organic Theater Co., Chicago, 1974; Regent Theatre, London, 1977	1974	1977
Squirrels, St Nicholas Theater Company, Chicago, 1974; King's Head Theatre, London, 1993	1974	1993
American Buffalo, Goodman Theater Company, Chicago, 1975; National Theatre, London, 1978	1975	1978
Reunion, St Nicholas Theater Company, Chicago, 1976	1976	
The Woods, St Nicholas Theater Company, Chicago, 1977	1977	
The Water Engine, St Nicholas Theater Company, Chicago, 1977; Hampstead Theatre, London, 1989	1977	1989
A Life in the Theatre, Goodman Theater, Chicago; Theatre de Lys, New York, 1977; Brighton, 1989	1977	1989
Mr Happiness, New York Shakespeare Festival, New York, 1978	1978	
Prairie du Chien, National Public Radio, 1979; Royal Court Theatre Upstairs, London, 1986	1979	1986
Lakeboat, Court Street Theater, Milwaukee Rep, Milwaukee, WI, 1980	1980	
Edmond, Goodman Theater, Chicago, 1982; Royal Court Theatre, London, 1985	1982	1985
The Disappearance of the Jews, Goodman Theater, Chicago, 1983	1983	
Glengarry Glen Ross, Goodman Theater, Chicago, 1984; National Theatre, London, 1983	1984	1983

Reunion

The Characters:

Carol Mindler, *twenty-four years old*
Bernie Cary, *her father*

The Scene: Bernie's apartment

The Time: Sunday afternoon in early March

Reunion was first produced by the St Nicholas Theater Company, Chicago, Illinois, on 9 January 1976, with the following cast:

Bernie Cary	Don Marston
Carol Mindler	Linda Kimbrough

Directed by Cecil O'Neal

The Yale Repertory production of *Reunion* opened in New Haven, Connecticut, on 14 October 1977, with the following cast:

Bernie Cary	Michael Higgins
Carol Mindler	Lindsay Crouse

Directed by Walt Jones
Set by Kate Edmunds
Lighting by William Connor

Reunion was first produced in the UK in a double bill with *Dark Pony* at the King's Head Theatre Club, London, in February 1981, directed by Stuart Owen, with the following cast:

Bernie Cary	Don Fellowes
Carol Mindler	Susannah Fellowes

Scene 1

Bernie I would of recognized you anywhere.
It is you. Isn't it?
Carol. Is that you?
You haven't changed a bit.
I would of recognized you anywhere . . .
This is a very important moment.
But there's no reason why we should have it in the hall so let
me take your coat . . .
I feel like a racehorse. You ever go to the track?
Well, that's what I feel like.
If I was still drinking, I'd offer you a drink.
If I was still drinking, you probably wouldn't be here.
That's all right.

Carol Bernie . . .

Bernie You're not going to call me Dad, or like that? . . .
Thank God.
So here we are.

Carol Yes.

Bernie So how you been?

Carol Fine.

Bernie Great.

Carol You?

Bernie Since the last time you saw me, mainly bad, lately
good. You look wonderful.

Carol You don't look so bad yourself. For an old man. You
take good care of yourself.

Bernie Well, I better. Who else is going to take care of
me? . . .
The VA, of course. They take pretty good care of me, I'm
forced to admit.

I still go to see them about three times a year for my back.
They take good care of you in the hospital.
The guys at AA, I don't see them much anymore.
Thank God. They took pretty good care of me.
I hated those sonofabitches . . .
Frank over at the place. He took care of me for a while.
Five there, ten here . . . he gave me a job.
Knows the restaurant business like the back of his hand.
I've been a very lucky guy.

Carol You've got a lot of friends, Bernie.

Bernie Always have.
For some reason.
You take pretty good care of yourself.

Carol Got to.

Bernie Yeah.

Carol The AA are the ones who put us in touch with you.
Gerry went.
He said they seemed like very nice people.

Bernie Very contrite.
You still go to church?

Carol No. Nobody goes to church anymore. (*Pause.*) You still go to church?

Bernie I never went to church. Since I was a kid.
Easter.

Carol We should both go.
Renew our faith.
Gerry goes to church.

Bernie Yeah? Does he mean it?

Carol Who knows.

Bernie He might mean it. You never know . . .
Some of 'em mean it.

Scene 2

Bernie Goddamn, it's good to see you.
It's good to see you.

Carol This apartment is very nice.

Bernie I did it myself. Leslie, my friend, she helped.
Quite a lot, actually . . . to put the place in the state it's in now.
But the basic place . . . I furnished it.
Fixed it up.
Been here two years plus . . .
I'm glad you like it.

Carol Our place is quite nice. You'll like it a lot.
When you come see it. You have to come out. Very soon.
I did it myself.
It's so comfortable.
It's a real home, you know?
It's just five rooms.
It gets a little cramped when the kids are there.
Gerry's kids.
They sleep in the living room . . .
They're good kids.
Gerry has a study.
We're very comfortable there.

Bernie You got a doorman?

Carol Yes . . .
The building's very safe.
Lots of light and air.
We're thinking of building a house. (*Pause.*)
This place really is lovely, Bernie.

Bernie What can I tell you.

Scene 3

Carol (*sees bomber group picture*) Are you in there?

Bernie Yeah.

Carol I'm going to pick you out.

Bernie That's a long time ago.

Carol (*indicates*) There!

Bernie That's me.
I haven't changed, huh?

Carol Bernie Cary. Army Air Corps.

Bernie Butch. They called me Butch then.

Carol Why?

Bernie . . . I couldn't tell you to save my life.
Those were strange times.

Carol What's this?

Bernie It's a medal.
Sit down. Sit down. It's nothing.
I fought. I did my bit.
If you want to know about your father
I was a tail gunner.
I shot a machine gun. Big deal.
They had a life expectancy of – you know what? – Three
missions. Three.
What the hell. You can get killed in a steel mill, right?
But I'm no hero.
They put you in a plane with a gun, it pays to shoot at the
guys who are trying to kill you.
Where's the courage in that . . .
But you didn't have to take anything.
From nobody.
That was all right.
Anybody get wise – some wiseass lieutenant – I say:
'Shove it, Champ. I'm a fuckin' tail gunner on a B-17,
and I don't take no shit from some chicken lieutenant.'

And I didn't. From Anybody.
So what does that make me.
You would like England.

Carol I've been there.

Bernie You've been there? What? With your new husband?

Carol With him and by myself.

Bernie Where else you been?

Carol Jamaica. Around the States.

Bernie See America First, huh?
I worked a year in San Francisco. In a body shop.

Carol I've been in San Francisco.

Bernie Some fine people in San Francisco.

Carol Oh, yes.

Bernie And a lot of assholes.

Carol Lot of assholes all over.

Bernie Aah, people are people, you know?
Tell me about your new husband.

Carol I want to know about you.

Bernie And I want to know about you.
So. Does he love you?
I swear I'll kill the sonofabitch, so tell me the truth.

Carol He loves me.

Bernie And you love him?

Carol Yes.

Bernie So where's the story in that?

Carol No story.
Just the usual.

Bernie So it's not 'the usual' for nothing.
These things work out. They work themselves out.
Is he a good guy?

Carol He's . . .
He's a good guy. I think he's frightened of women.

Bernie He's frightened of you? . . .
That's funny.
But you know, never having been a man, you don't know –
but a lot of men are frightened of women,
let me tell you.
Beautiful women especially can be frightening.
There's no shame in that.
He takes good care of you.

Carol Yes.

Bernie So what do you want?

Carol I want to hear about you.

Bernie What's to tell? You see it all here. Have a look.
Fifty-three years old.
Ex-alcoholic.
Ex-this.
Ex-that.
Democrat.
You smoke pot?

Carol No. You?

Bernie Nope.
Tried it once. Don't like the taste.
When I was a drunk I never drank anything but the best.
Saw no reason to change my style of life simply because I
happened to be an alcoholic.
Taste . . .
Never bummed for change. Waste of time.
Bill. Two bills, bounce a check.
Respectable.
If you're a drunk, you'd better be respectable . . .
1951 I lost my license. Fourteen citations for drunk driving in
the month of December 1951.
You were what? Four.
I was living on the Cape.
You and your mother were in Newton.

Carol What were you doing?

Bernie In 1951 I was in the Vet's Hospital awhile with my back.
The rest of the time I was working for the Phone Company.
Worked for the Phone Company ten years.
I was seeing this girl in Boston.
Your mother and I were split . . .
I got that court order in 1951.
You know . . .
Did you know I wanted to see you?
Did they tell you anything?
I wanted to come see you, you know.
I couldn't see you because of that court order.

Carol I don't know. They told me . . . something.

Bernie (*pause*) I was a mover for a year.
Cross country.
I missed my brother's funeral. Your Uncle Alex.
You never met him. Did you ever meet Alex?

Carol Yes.

Bernie He's dead now. 1962.
And his wife, Lorraine, won't talk to me since I missed his funeral.
I'm sorry I missed it, too. But what the hell.
Life goes on. And when he died I was out west someplace with American Van Lines and I didn't even know about it 'til September . . .
You wanna hear a story?

Carol Sure do.

Bernie I'll tell you a story. So I'd been drunk at the time for several years and was walking down Tremont Street one evening around nine and here's this big van in front of a warehouse and the driver is ringing the bell in the shipping dock trying to get in (which he won't do, because they moved a couple of weeks ago and the warehouse is deserted. But he doesn't know that).
So I say, 'Hey, you looking for Hub City Transport?' And he

says yeah, and I tell him they're over in Lechmere. So he says
'Where?' So I tell him I don't know the address but I can take
him there. Which was, of course, a bunch of shit, but I
figured maybe I could make a couple of bucks on the deal.
And why not.
So I ride over to Lechmere.
I find the warehouse.
You ever been to Lechmere?

Carol Just passing through.

Bernie Very depressing.
So, anyway. He's in Lechmere to pick up a load.
And he offers me ten bucks to help him load the van.
So fine. Later we go across the street for a cup of coffee and he
gives me this story. He just fired his partner, he likes the way
I handle furniture, and do I want a job?
Hey, what the hell.
We finish the coffee and off we go.
And for one year I didn't get home, never shaved, wore the
same goddamn clothes, slept in the cab, made some money,
spent some money, saw the country. Alex died, and I missed
his funeral.
Which, of course, is why Lorraine won't talk to me.
Because I got back in September and I'm back a day or so
and I go over to Alex's.
Lorraine answers the door and I tell her,
'Lorraine, tell your fat-ass husband to grab his coat because
we are gong to the track.' He loved the track.
And she says: 'If I ever catch you in my sight again, drunk or
sober, I'm going to punch your fucking heart out.'
Which were harsh words for her.
And to this day – she believed I was in town and drunk at the
time of the funeral – not once have I seen or spoken to her in
ten years . . .
And we were very close at one time.
She was a good woman.
Very loyal . . .
Alex fought in the war.
What the hell. How's your mother?

Carol Good.

Bernie What about the guy she married?

Carol Good.
You know, he's a hell of a man.

Bernie No! Don't doubt it for a second. I never met the sonofabitch, but I'd stake my life on it . . .
You got any kids?

Carol No.

Bernie Didn't think so. How long you been married?

Carol Two years. Gerry's got two kids.

Bernie You told me. How old?

Carol Twelve and eight. Boys.

Bernie How are they?

Carol They're good boys.

Bernie You like 'em?

Carol We get along.

Bernie They like you?

Carol You know how it is.

Bernie Their other mother died?

Carol Divorced.

Bernie . . . I like him, Gerry. He seems like an all right guy. A thoughtful guy . . .
Jesus, he gave me a moment, though.
I come into the restaurant and Frank – Frank's the owner – he says, 'Bernie, there's a guy outside askin' for Butch Cary.' Now, I haven't called myself Butch since I'm on the wagon, three years.
I was called Butch from the days in the Air Corps, and all my old drunk partners know me as Butch. So. I figure it's some old acquaintance looking for a handout, or a bill collector. Because he called me Butch.
So I peek out the kitchen door and there's this real nice-

looking guy around forty – what am I telling you what he
looks like –
Anyway, it's obvious he's not a bill collector, and he's not
looking for a handout, and I don't know him from Adam.
So I get out of the kitchen – he probably told you this stuff –
I still got my coat on 'cause I just walked in the back
door . . .
I guess I looked kind of suspicious – who wouldn't – and I go
over to him and he says, 'Are you Butch Cary?'
And I say, 'Yeah, who are you?'
He says, 'I'm Gerry Mindler. I'm Carol's husband. Your
daughter.'
I told him I know who my daughter is.
I told him, 'Mister, I am one tough sonofabitch, but I'll be
goddamned if I don't feel like I'm gonna bust out crying.'
And I almost did.

Scene 4

Bernie You got a brother you never met, you know, a half-
brother. Marty.
My and Ruth's kid. Ruth, my second wife. You could call her
your stepmother . . . if it made any sense.
I know your mother had another daughter.

Carol Barbara.

Bernie I know.

Carol We're very close.

Bernie I don't doubt it.

Carol We are.

Bernie Marty. You'd like him.

Carol How is he?

Bernie I haven't seen him now in several years. He's say
three years younger than you. He's a good kid.

Carol What does he do?

Bernie Do?
The last time I heard – and this might of changed – nothing.

Carol What was Ruth like?

Bernie Like your mother, I'm sorry to say.
Not that she wasn't a lovely woman.
And not that your . . .

Carol . . . It's okay.

Bernie Anyway, we didn't get along too long. And your
mother was not such a hotshot either, to get down to it.
Ruth never understood me. I take it back, she understood
me. When Marty was young. We got along.

Carol And then?

Bernie I left her. These things happen.
But, Jesus, he was a fine little kid.
Having kids, Carol, is something no one can describe.
Having your own kids is . . . indescribable.
I mean it.
You were quite a little kid.
We used to have a good time.
Going to the zoo . . .
Do you remember that? Do you remember what you used to
say when I came home?
Three years old?
I'd come in the door.
You'd say: 'Hi there, Pop!'
I don't know where you picked that up. I guess your mother
used to coach you.
Do you remember that?
Do you remember going to the Science Museum?
We used to be over there every week. See the locomotive . . .
The steam engines, you remember that?
You were a beautiful kid.
You were everything to your mother and me.
I still got the pictures.
You want to see how cute you were? You wait here.
Just sit there.

You know who took those? Alex took those at his house . . .
Fourth of July 1950. It was the first year he had his new
house.
You probably don't remember.
Took them with his Brownie.
You were crying for some reason, and I said, 'Look at the
camera, baby . . .' I'll be goddamned if I know where those
pictures are.

Carol It's okay.

Bernie They're around here somewhere.

Carol It's okay, Bernie.

Bernie But where can they be?
I look at 'em constantly . . .
You want some coffee?

Carol No, thanks.

Bernie You smoke too much.

Carol I know it.

Bernie Your husband smoke?

Carol Yes.

Bernie Does he tell you to cut down?

Carol Yes.

Bernie They're no good for you.

Carol I know.

Bernie He should set an example.

Carol He's my husband, Bernie, not my father.

Bernie I don't smoke.
I gave it up.
When I went on the wagon.
Did I tell you I'm thinking about getting married again?

Carol No.

Bernie It's not definite. Not yet.
I'm just thinking.
Leslie. She works at the restaurant. Gerry met her.

Carol Tell me about her.

Bernie . . . She knows me. I know her.
I respect her.
She's a good worker, she knows my past.
I think she loves me. She's about forty . . .
Was married once.
It's like a habit.
How would you, you know . . . feel if I got married again?
Would that . . . do anything to you?
I realize you don't have a long basis for comparison.

Carol I think it would be good for you.

Bernie You think that, huh?

Carol Yes.

Bernie Of course it wouldn't get in the way of our getting to
know each other.

Carol Why are you getting married again?

Bernie . . . Companionship.

Scene 5

Bernie But I'm a happy man now. And I don't use the term
loosely.
I got a good job at the restaurant.
I've stopped drinking. I'm putting a little money away.

Carol I'm glad to hear it.

Bernie Well, there's nothing wrong with it.
For the first time in a long time I get a kick out of what I'm
doing.
I enjoy it at work. Everybody knows me. They respect me.
I spend a lot of time walking. Just walking in the Common.

After all this time. Not to cadge a drink. Or to get laid.
Excuse me . . .
People always talk about going out to the country or getting
back to nature and all the time I say, 'Yeah, yeah,' and what
does it mean?
I see the logic of it, but it means nothing to me.
Because my entire life I'm looking for a way around.
Do you know what I mean?
Like drinking, certainly, or with your mother, or my second
wife . . . Being in debt – there was never a reason for all that
money trouble – and changing jobs all the time . . . so what
does it get me but dumber and dumber, and I'm a cynic.
But now . . .
On the other hand, it's about time – I mean, I'm fifty-three
years old. I've spent the majority of my life drinking and,
when you come right down to it, being a hateful
sonofabitch . . .
But you, married. Living well. You live well.
A nice guy. A fine guy for a husband.
Going to have . . . maybe . . . kids.
You shouldn't let it bother you, but you have a lot of
possibilities. Don't you feel that?

Carol I do.

Bernie Well, then. The rest is not very important. It's for
the weaklings.
No, really. And I like people as much as the next guy.
It's for the sissies and the drinkers – which I was – who need
it.
Otherwise . . . What have you got to lose?
Take a chance.
You got to take your chance for happiness.
You got to grab it.
You got to know it and you got to want it.
And you got to *take* it.
Because all the possessions in the world can't take it for you.
Do you know what I'm talking about? . . .
It's a fucking jungle out there. And you got to learn the rules
because *nobody's* going to learn them for you.

You wanna drink? Go drink.
You wanna do *this?* Pay the price.
Always the price. Whatever it is.
And you gotta know it and be prepared to pay it if you don't
want it to pass you by.
And if you don't know that, you gotta find it out, and that's
all I know.

Scene 6

Bernie I don't care.
1950, 1970. (*Pause.*)
You know what I mean.
What's on my mind now is getting to know you.
And maybe getting married again.
You look good. Jesus, you are a good-looking young woman.

Carol I get it all from you.

Bernie Aaah . . .

Carol I used to think you were the handsomest man I ever
saw.
You used to look just like Tonto.

Bernie Tonto?

Carol The Indian. The Lone Ranger's friend.

Bernie I know who Tonto is.

Carol It was my secret. I was sure you were Tonto.
I asked you once.
You remember?

Bernie No.

Carol You said, 'No, of course not.'
I was very upset. I didn't know why you were lying to me.

Bernie I'm sorry.

Carol I was about four.
I never told anyone.

I thought that it was our secret. (*Pause.*)
You wanted me to keep our secret. (*Pause.*)

Bernie Thank you.

Carol Bernie . . .

Bernie What?

Carol Bernie, you're wasted in the restaurant. Do you know that?

Bernie I like it at the restaurant.
I love it at the restaurant.
It's where I work. Leslie works there.
What do you mean?

Carol I mean . . .

Bernie I mean who do you think you're talking to? This is not Tonto the Indian but Butch Cary, ex-drunk.
The only two worthwhile things I ever did in my life were work for the Phone Company and fire a machine gun, and I can't do either of them anymore, not that I feel sorry for myself, but I'm just telling you.
I mean I am what I am and that's what happiness comes from . . . being just that. Don't you agree? . . . I mean you must remember that your mother was a very different sort of person from me. As is, I'm sure, the guy she married. And the way you're brought up, though all very well and good . . . is not basically my life, as fine as it may be and I hope it brings you a lot of happiness.
I mean, you haven't even *been* to the restaurant, for chrissakes . . .
It's very clean and . . .

Carol No, I'm sure it's . . . I only meant . . .

Bernie I know what you meant.
I know what you're talking about.
But lookit, my life needn't be your life in any sense of the word, you know?
I like it like I am, and if you find that the people you . . . go with, your friends and so on . . .

Carol Don't be silly, Bernie.

Bernie I'm not being silly.

Carol Yes, you are, and that's the last I want to say about it.

Bernie Okay, but . . .

Carol So for chrissakes, knock it off, okay?

Scene 7

Bernie I gotta admit it. I knew you were coming over. I was scared.

Carol Yes, me too.

Bernie There's nothing wrong in that.

Carol No.

Bernie After all, what were we going to expect . . .
Red Sails in the Sunset? . . .
What do you do now? I mean . . .

Carol I work for Gerry. At the Office.

Bernie You're a secretary?

Carol I'm just kind of . . . everything.

Bernie It sounds great.

Carol It actually has a lot of responsibility.

Bernie As long as you like it, right?

Carol (*pause*) Right.

Bernie So quit . . .
Anyway, it's not the end of the world.

Carol No (*Pause.*) No. (*Pause.*) We're not . . . sleeping together much anymore.

Bernie Oh.

Carol And that's only *part* of it.

Bernie What's the rest of it? (*Pause*.)
Come on, let me tell you something. You know what my advice to you is?
'Don't let it get you down.'

Carol He's not such a great lover, anyway.

Bernie He seems like a nice enough guy.

Carol He's a lousy fuck.

Bernie That doesn't mean he isn't a nice guy, Carol.

Carol What do you know about it?

Bernie Speaking as your father and as a guy with quite an experience of the world . . .

Carol . . . whatever . . .

Bernie . . . not a hell of a lot. But I'll tell you, he's genuinely fond of you . . .
That's got to count for something . . .
Right?

Scene 8

Carol You know – when I was young they used to talk about Broken Homes.
Today, nothing. Everyone's divorced. Every kid on the block's got three sets of parents.
But . . .
It's got to have affected my marriage . . .
I came from a Broken Home.
The most important institution in America.

Bernie Life goes on. Your mother and me . . .

Carol . . . Oh, yeah, life goes on. And no matter how much of an asshole you may be, or may have been, life goes on.
Gerry's like that.

Bernie I'm not going to lie to you. I felt guilt and remorse and every other goddamn thing. I missed you.

What the hell.
I was mad. I was mad at your mother. I was mad at you.
I was mad at the fucking government that never treated me
like anything but a little kid . . . saving their ass with
daylight precision bombing . . .
Everybody hates the VA.
I mean, understand: I'm not asking you to understand me,
Carol, because we've both been through enough.
Am I right?

Pause.

Carol Gerry was in Korea.

Bernie Yes? And what does he have to say about it?

Carol Nothing.

Scene 9

Bernie Let me tell you a story.
One time – this was strange – when I'm working for the
Phone Company. I'm out on the Cape. Lineman.
Repairs, on the street. I'm making out okay, what with that
and my disability.
Bought myself a new Buick.
Beautiful sonofabitch. Used to drive into Boston and go out
to Wonderland with Alex.
He loved that car. I think he was secretly envious.
And so I'm working out on the Cape. It's December
thirtieth.
I get invited to a New Year's party in Provincetown. I'm
supposed to be working.
So I call in sick. What the hell, I had a good work record.
And it's New Year's Eve day and I'm getting ready to drive
to Provincetown.
Put a hundred bucks in my wallet and I go to Mitchell's –
that's the tavern in Falmouth I used to hang out at – and
there's this Italian kid shooting pool. About twenty. I don't
know . . . Steve, something like that.

So I offer him twenty bucks to drive out to Provincetown
with me, stay in the car, and drive me home New Year's Day.
So fine. We get up to Provincetown, I go over to Kenny's
house . . . Kenny Hill. You would of liked him. He would
have liked you, I can tell you that. Had an eye for younger
women. Who could blame him.
And so we had a hell of a party.
That's one thing Kenny knew how to do is throw a party.
But the point is not the party but the next morning.
So the next morning I get up off the couch or wherever I was
and put on my coat and go out to the car to invite this kid
Steve in for a cup of coffee or something.
So there's the Buick but the kid is gone. Nowhere to be found.
Vanished. Along with my flashlight, which I don't find out
'til I rack the car up near Truro. (*Pause.*) But hold on. (*He
thinks for a moment.*)
I think he took my flashlight . . . (*Pause.*)
So I go back in the house. Get myself together, and I figure
I'd better start back to Falmouth. I'm hung over as a
sonofabitch. I say goodbye to my friends, grab a bottle, and
into the car.
It's snowing up a storm. I can hardly see anyway. I'm
weaving all over the road. Next thing I know I'm asleep.
And the following thing I'm wrapped around a telephone
pole.
So I get out. Knocked the pole clean over; the hood of the
Buick is wrenched to shit. I go to get out the flashlight to try
to get a look at the engine, and the flashlight's gone.
There's no help for it, so I get back in and go to sleep.
Next thing I know here comes a Black and White. The cop
wakes me up, I happen to know him from around Falmouth,
and I convince him that it's all an accident, and I give him a
drink and he drives me home and promises to call the garage.
So you should be careful who you're calling a pig.
Any case, I no sooner get in bed than ten seconds later,
Wham! The telephone rings and it's Jim Daugherty, the
supervisor for the Cape.
'How are you feeling?' he asks.
'Like a big piece of cow shit,' I tell him.

'You gotta come in today,' he says.
'Jim,' I tell him, 'I'm sick, it's New Year's, get someone else.'
'Everybody else is drunk,' he says, 'I'm the only one here,
and some asshole knocked down a pole near Truro.'
. . . So I tell him my car won't start. He says he's coming over
in the truck to get me.
So I make some coffee and he comes and we go over to Truro
to fix the pole.
He's cursing the whole way:
'Jagoff' this and 'Asshole' that . . .
And what with the overtime and holiday pay and the twenty
Jim slipped me for coming along I made about ninety bucks
for one afternoon. And Jim was so mad, he did most of the
work himself and I spent most of the time in the cab drinking.

Scene 10

Bernie But I can't work for the Phone Company anymore.
When they finally pulled my license, that was it.
I hit a cop car. Actually it sounds more exciting than it was.
It was an unmarked car. He was parked anyway. Only time
I ever got a ticket in Boston. A heartbreaker.
Anyway, I lost my license and that was it. I got fired and they
meant it.
Jim Daugherty went down to Boston to talk to 'em.
No Dice.
He even wrote a letter to the Board of Trustees for me.
The Board of Trustees of the Phone Company.
No good.
He said if I got fired he was going to quit, too.
. . . He didn't, though . . .
But he would've . . .
Broke him up, too. Best goddamn lineman on the Cape.
Eight years, best record.
We were very close . . .
Canned. Like that. Pension, benefits, seniority.
Shot . . .

It was probably for the best.
But I'll be goddamned if I can see how.
I used to drink a bit on the job. But who didn't?
Jim knew that. Nobody cared.
If it hadn't showed up in the accident report, I'd be
working today.
What the hell.

Carol How long till you can get your license back?

Bernie Supposedly never, but, actually, in about a year.
They review it.
They told me about it at the AA. The guys there go up with
you.
Their opinion is very respected.

Carol I was a teacher for a while.

Bernie You were? Where?

Carol In Newton. I taught sixth grade.

Bernie How about that! Where?

Carol At the Horace Mann School.

Bernie You were at the Horace Mann School?

Carol For a year and a half.

Bernie And I was right across the street?

Carol Where?

Bernie At the Garage.
The Company Garage is right across the street. I was out
there all the time.
We used to eat at Mike's. Did you ever go in there?

Carol No. I went in for cigarettes once in a while.

Bernie I used to go in there all the time. I was there – easily
– twice a week.
For years.
Goddamn.
When were you there?

Carol 1969.

Bernie . . . I haven't worked for the Phone Company since '55.
You want some tea?

Carol You have any coffee?

Bernie Yeah, sure. Instant.

Carol That's fine.

Bernie But I bet I saw you around. Boston, Boylston Street . . .

Carol We must've seen each other . . . in the Common . . . A hundred times.

Scene 11

Bernie I remember the day you turned twenty-one.
February fourth, 1968.
Your birthday.
I was going to call you up.
You probably don't believe it.
It's not important.
The actions are important.
The present is important.
I spent a couple of days in jail once.
What it taught me, you've gotta be where you are.
. . . While you're there.
Or you're nowhere.
Do you know what I mean?
As it pertains to you and me?
Because I think it's very important . . .
Does this make any sense to you?

Carol I want to get to know you.

Bernie And I want to get to know you. But that's not going to magically wipe out twenty years . . .
In which you were growing up, which you had to do anyway, and I was drunk . . .

I don't mean to get stupid about it.
But let's get up, go out, do this, go look at the locomotive if
they've still got it there, something . . . you know?
Because, all kidding aside, what's between us isn't going
nowhere, and the rest of it doesn't exist.

Scene 12

Bernie So let me ask you something – you don't mind if I get
personal for a second, do you?

Carol What? (*Pause.*)

Bernie What I want to know is why all of a sudden you
come looking for me. And it's not that I'm criticizing you.

Carol Why should I think you were criticizing me?

Pause.

Bernie I mean, I could of come looking for *you* after you
were twenty-one. Not that I was sure how you'd feel about
seeing me . . . but you must of felt the same way? No.
I mean, it must of been . . . I'm guessing . . . some kind of
decision to get you to all of a sudden come looking for me.
How did you find me?

Carol Through the AA.

Bernie And you just kind of decided and sent Gerry over to
meet me?

Carol Yes.

Bernie And why now?

Carol I felt lonely.

Bernie . . . Oh. (*Pause.*)

Carol You're my father.

Scene 13

Carol I feel lonely.

Pause.

Bernie Who doesn't?

Carol Do you?

Bernie Sometimes.

Carol I feel cheated.
And, do you know what? I never had a father.

Bernie Carol . . .

Carol And I don't want to be pals and buddies; I want you to be my father. (*Pause.*)
And to hear your goddamn war stories and the whole thing.
And that's why now because that's how I feel. (*Pause.*)
I'm entitled to it.
Am I?
Am I?

Bernie Yes.

Carol I am. You're goddamn right.

Bernie You know what the important thing is?

Carol What?

Bernie To be together.
What's past is in the past . . . it's gone.
You're a grown woman . . . I'm on the wagon, your mother's remarried, I got a good job, and there's no reason . . .
I can't make it up to you.

Carol Do you have to go to work tonight?

Bernie I don't work on Sundays. But Sandy got sick so I was supposed to come in but I called Frank and he told me he'd get someone else to cover so I don't have to go in tonight.
You want to do something?

Carol Gerry was . . . he said he'd like it if we went out to dinner.
Would you like that?

Bernie Yeah. I'd like that.

Carol We could go out by ourselves if you want.

Bernie No. It's a good idea I think.
And it's no big thing in any case, right?

Carol . . . We could go out, just the two of us.

Bernie Whatever you want. What you want, Carol. That's what we'll do.

Scene 14

Bernie I got you something. Sit down. I'll give it to you.

Carol What is it?

Bernie I don't know. I found it on the bus.

Carol . . . It's beautiful.

Bernie Yeah.

Carol (*reading inscription*) 'To Carol from her Father. March eighth, 1973.'

Bernie It's my fault. It's not their fault. My threes look like eights.
It's only five days off.
It's the thought that counts . . .
Ruth told me that you should never give anyone jewelry because then they'll always think they have to wear it when you're around . . .
So I never gave her any.

Carol It's real gold . . .
Thank you, Bernie.

Bernie I'm not going to tell you you don't have to wear it if you don't like it.
I hope you do like it.

Carol I do like it . . .

Bernie So what's the weather like out there?

Carol It's fine. Just a little chilly.

Bernie We should be getting ready, no? Shouldn't you call Gerry?

Carol Yes.

Bernie So you do that and I'll put away the things and then we'll go.

Carol The bracelet's lovely, Bernie.

Bernie Thank you.

Dark Pony

This play is dedicated to Lindsay Crouse

The Characters:

The Father
The Daughter

The Scene: An automobile

The Time: Night

Dark Pony opened on 14 October 1977, in a Yale Repertory production, New Haven, Connecticut, with the following cast:

The Father   Michael Higgins
The Daughter   Lindsay Crouse

Directed by Walt Jones
Set by Kate Edmunds
Lighting by William Connor

Dark Pony was first produced in the UK in a double bill with *Reunion* at the King's Head Theatre Club, London, in February 1981, directed by Stuart Owen, with the following cast:

The Father   Don Fellowes
The Daughter   Susannah Fellowes

Father Once upon a time there was an Indian. (*Pause.*)
In the days when wild things roamed the land, and long
before the White Man came here.

Daughter When was this?

Father A long, long time ago. (*Pause.*)

Daughter (*to self*) Long ago.

Father He was a Brave, and very handsome.

Daughter What's a Brave?

Father A man who fights in war.
A young man.
And his body was like Iron.
and he could see like an Eagle.
And he could run like a Deer.
You ever see a deer run?

Daughter Sure.

Father And swim like a fish.

Daughter And he ran like a deer?

Father Yes.

Daughter Hopping?

Father No. Not hopping. But as fast as deer run when they
run.

Daughter And could he hop a fence?

Father He could jump over it. Yes.

Daughter (*to self*) Good.

Father His name was . . .

Father *and* **Daughter** (*simultaneously*) Rain Boy.

Father And he was beloved by all his tribe,
because he was both brave and gay.

And he brought happiness to all around him just by smiling.
If the times were bad.
Or singing songs he used to sing.
Or telling stories.
Then he would act out the parts.
He was a renowned fighter.

Daughter Who did they fight?

Father Other tribes.

Daughter The Germans?

Father No.
And Rain Boy had a special friend.

Daughter I know.

Father Who?

Daughter Dark Pony!

Father Yes, Dark Pony.
When he was in trouble or whenever he found that he needed help,
then he would call his friend Dark Pony.
He would say:
'Dark Pony . . .'

Father *and* **Daughter** (*simultaneously*) 'Dark Pony, your friend Rain Boy calls to you.'

Father Then he'd look up, if they were down in a valley, or around, if they were in a culvert, or a stream; or if they were high on a meadow.
He would see a speck. A dark red speck . . .

Daughter (*to self*) Like blood.

Father Red. Like a rose – like sunset in the wheat or grass.
Galloping towards him. (*Pause.*)
Dark Pony.
Come to help him.

Daughter (*to self*) 'Your friend Rain Boy calls to you.'

Father If he was wounded, pick him up and carry him away upon his back.
If he was thirsty, bring him cool stream water in a hide.
If he was hungry, bring him food.

Daughter (*to self*) Something to eat.

Father One day he was bound home after many moons of fighting in a foreign province.
He had not seen his wife or baby in a long, long while.

Daughter (*to self*) He missed them.

Father And he longed to see her.
Up they went.
Up through the mountains.
Climbing home.
Until the snows came.
Falling early on the homebound Braves –
It trapped them.

Daughter (*to self*) In the snow.

Father Up in the mountains.
Cold.
Alone.
Until his enemies all stole away one night;
they took his food, and told his friends that he had died, and crept on through the mountain 'til he was alone. (*Pause.*)
In the mountain woods. (*Pause.*)
Starved and weak.
As he trudged on alone to see his young wife and his child.
Many days.
Until one night when he had fallen and was set upon by wolves.

Daughter No!

Father He had built a fire so he could rest, and when it burnt down he would rise and march again.

Daughter (*to self*) This was in Winter.

Father When he woke, what did he see? The eyes of *wolves*!

Daughter (*to self*) No.

Father Glaring at him from the darkness. Orange eyes and howling.

Daughter I'm scared.

Pause.

Father And they drew closer.
He cried out with all his strength:
'Dark Pony, Dark Pony, your friend, Rain Boy, calls to you.'
And he looked up.
But he was alone.
The wolves came closer.
He cried:
'Dark Pony, Dark Pony.
Your friend, Rain Boy, calls to you.'
The wolves stopped. (*Pause.*)
He lifted up a log from the fire to defend himself, but he knew
that he couldn't last long.
He could smell them now. (*Pause.*)
They came closer.
'Oh,' he said. (*Pause.*)
'Oh, Dark Pony . . .' (*Pause.*)
'You have forgotten me.'
Then he heard neighing. (*Pause.*)
Hooves beating through the snow.
From the highest cliff.
Down through the mountain.
Crying. And galloping.
Borne like the sleet on the wind.
As he fell back exhausted,
the wolves whined.
They tried to flee.

Daughter (*to self*) They tried to leave.

Father But he bore down upon them. (*Pause.*)
And through their midst. (*Pause.*)
Through the dying fire.
The snow grew red with their blood. (*Pause.*)

Then all became quiet.
The wind blew.
The snow drifted.
He lay in silence.
He had become cold.
Dark Pony walked over to him, and he nudged him with his
nose. (*Pause.*)
And he neighed. (*Pause.*)
And he licked his face. (*Pause.*)
Slowly he opened his eyes. (*Pause.*)
He looked up above him.
Dark Pony was standing there. (*Pause.*)
'Oh, Dark Pony,' he said . . . (*Pause.*)
'I thought you had forgotten me.' (*Pause.*)

Daughter Are we almost home yet?

Father Yes. (*Pause.*)
(*To self.*) Down from the mountains.
Down.
Across the hills.
Across the prairies.

Daughter . . . Because I remember how it sounds.

Father You do?

Daughter The road.

Father Yes.
We are almost there.

Daughter (*to self*) 'Cause I remember how it sounds.

Father . . . Down in the Valleys – he would look above and
see his friend there.

Daughter (*to self*) . . . Just before we get home.

Pause.

Father (*to self*) 'Dark Pony,
Rain Boy calls to you.'

Pause.

Daughter We are almost home.

A Life in the Theatre

We counterfeited once for your disport
Men's joy and sorrow; but our day has passed.
We pray you pardon all where we fell short –
Seeing we were your servants to this last.

— Rudyard Kipling
'Actors'

This play is dedicated to Gregory Mosher

The Characters:

Robert, *an older actor*
John, *a younger actor*

The Scene: Various spots around a theater

The scenes in this play can be divided into onstage and backstage scenes. In the onstage scenes, we see John and Robert portraying characters in various plays in the repertory theater for which they work. A beautiful solution for staging *A Life in the Theatre* in a proscenium house was arrived at by Michael Merritt and Gregory Mosher, the play's first designer and director, respectively, in their production at the Goodman Theater Stage Two, in Chicago. They decided that it might be provocative if a second curtain were installed upstage, behind which the audience for whom John and Robert play their onstage scenes sits. This curtain is opened when John and Robert work onstage, which is to say, playing in a play. Thus we see the actors' backs during their onstage scenes, and a full view of them during the backstage scenes – in effect, a true view from backstage.

A Life in the Theatre was first produced by the Theater de Lys, New York City, and opened on 20 October 1977, with the following cast:

John   Peter Evans
Robert   Ellis Rabb

Directed by Gerald Gutierrez
Set by John Lee Beatty
Lighting by Pat Collins

The New York production of *A Life in the Theatre* included a silent character, the Stage Manager, played by Benjamin Hendrickson.

A Life in the Theatre was first produced in the UK by Open Space Theatre in July 1979, directed by Alan Pearlman, with the following cast:

Robert   Freddie Jones
John   Patrick Ryecart

The play was produced at the Theatre Royal, Haymarket, in October 1989, directed by Bill Bryden, with the following cast:

Robert   Denholm Elliott
John   Samuel West

Scene 1

Backstage, after a performance.

Robert Goodnight, John.

John Goodnight.

Robert I thought the bedroom scene tonight was brilliant.

John Did you?

Robert Yes, I did. (*Pause.*) Didn't you think it went well?

John *shrugs.*

Robert Well, I thought it went brilliantly.

John Thank you.

Robert I wouldn't tell you if it wasn't so.

Pause.

John Thank you.

Robert Not at all. I wouldn't say it if it weren't so.

John The show went well tonight.

Robert I think it did.

John They were very bright.

Robert Yes. They were.

John It was . . .

Pause.

Robert What?

John An intelligent house. Didn't you feel?

Robert I did.

John They were very attentive.

Robert Yes. (*Pause.*) They were acute.

John Mmm.

Robert Yes. (*Pause.*) They were discerning.

John I thought they were.

Robert Perhaps they saw the show tonight (*Pause.*) on another level. Another, what? another . . . plane, eh? On another level of meaning. Do you know what I mean?

John I'm not sure I do.

Robert A plane of meaning.

Pause.

John A plane.

Robert Yes. I feel perhaps they saw a better show than the one we rehearsed.

John Mmm.

Robert Yes. What are you doing tonight?

John What am I doing now?

Robert Yes.

John Going out.

Robert Mmm.

Pause.

John For dinner.

Robert Yes.

John I'm famished.

Robert Yes.

John I haven't had an appetite for several days.

Robert Well, we've opened now.

John Yes. (*Pause.*) I'm hungry.

Robert Good.

Pause.

John It almost makes me feel . . .

Robert Go on.

John As if I'd earned the right . . . (*Pause.*) I was going to say 'to eat', but I'm not sure that that is what I really meant.

Robert What *did* you mean?

John A show like tonight's show . . .

Robert Yes?

John Going out there . . .

Robert Yes, go on.

John It makes me feel fulfilled.

Robert Ah. (*Pause.*) Well, it can do that.

Pause.

John I liked your scene.

Robert You did.

John Yes.

Robert Which scene?

John The courtroom.

Robert You liked that?

John Yes.

Robert I felt it was off tonight.

John You didn't.

Robert Yes.

John It wasn't off to me.

Robert Mmm.

John It did not seem off to me.

Robert I felt that it was off.

John If you were off you didn't look it.

Robert No?

John No.

Robert Mmm.

John The *doctor* scene . . .

Robert Yes?

John . . . may have been a trifle . . .

Robert Yes?

John Well . . .

Robert Say it. What? The doctor scene was what?

Pause.

John Brittle.

Pause.

Robert You thought that it was brittle?

John Well, I could be wrong.

Robert I trust your judgment.

John No, I could be wrong. I have been out-of-sorts . . . my eating habits haven't been . . . they've been a little . . .

Robert And you found it brittle, eh?

John Perhaps. I may have found it so. A bit.

Robert *Overly* brittle?

John No, not necessarily.

Pause.

Robert The whole scene?

John No, no. No. Not the whole scene, no.

Robert What then?

John A part. A part of it, perhaps.

Robert I wish that you would tell me if you found the whole scene so.

John It's only an opinion (of a portion of the scene)* and, in the last analysis, we're talking about a *word* . . .

Pause.

---

*Some portions of the dialogue appear in parentheses, which serve to mark a slight change of outlook on the part of the speaker – perhaps a momentary change to a more introspective regard. D.M.

Robert Yes.

John I'm sorry if I sounded . . .

Robert Not at all. I value your opinion.

John Yes. I know you do.

Robert Young people in the theatre . . . tomorrow's leaders . . .

Pause.

John Yes.

Robert Both of us, or was it only me?

John Of course not. I told you that I thought *you* were superb. (*Pause.*) *She* was off.

Robert You felt that too, eh?

John How could I not?

Robert I know. You felt that, eh?

John I did.

Robert Specifically tonight.

John Perhaps tonight especially.

Robert Yes. (*Pause.*) Especially tonight.

John Yes.

Robert Interesting. (*Pause.*) Yes.

John To me it's a marvel you can work with her at all. (*Pause.*) But to work with her so *well* . . .

Robert You do the best you can.

John It's enviable.

Robert The show goes on.

John I find much in that I must admire.

Robert Well, thank you.

John Not at all.

Pause.

Robert You have a job to do. You do it by your lights, you bring your expertise to bear, your sense of rightness . . . fellow feelings . . . etiquette . . . professional procedure . . . there are tools one brings to bear . . . procedure.

John No, it's quite inspiring.

Robert Thank you. (*Pause.*) The mugging is what gets me, eh?

John Mmm.

Robert Stilted diction and the pregnant pauses I can live with.

John Yes.

Robert The indicating and the mincing, these are fine, I can accept them.

John Yes.

Robert But the mugging . . .

John Yes.

Robert It rots my heart to look at it.

John I know.

Robert No soul . . . no humanism.

John No.

Robert No fellow-feeling.

John No.

Robert I want to kill the cunt.

John Don't let it worry you.

Robert It doesn't worry me. It just offends my sense of fitness.

John Mmm.

Robert If I could do her in and be assured I'd get away with it, I'd do it with a clear and open heart.

Pause.

John Mmm.

Robert That she should be allowed to live (not just to *live*
. . . but to parade around a stage . . .)

John Yes.

Robert And be *paid* for it . . .

John I totally agree with you.

Robert She would make *anyone* look brittle.

John Mmm.

Robert You bring me the man capable of looking flexible
the moment that she (or those of her ilk) walk on stage.

John I can't.

Robert No formal training.

John No.

Robert No sense of right and wrong.

John She exploits the theater.

Robert She does.

John She capitalizes on her beauty.

Pause.

Robert What beauty?

John Her attractiveness.

Robert Yes.

John It isn't really beauty.

Robert No.

John Beauty comes from within.

Robert Yes, I feel it does.

John She trades on it.

Robert She'll find out. (*Pause.*) Perhaps.

John It is a marvel you can work with her.

Robert It's not a marvel, John, you learn. You learn control. (*Pause.*) Character. A sense of right from wrong.

John Yes.

Pause.

Robert I tune her out.

John Mmm.

Robert When we're on stage, she isn't there for me.

John Mmmm.

Pause.

Robert How'd you like the table scene?

John I loved it.

Robert My, that scene was *fun* tonight.

John It looked it.

Robert Oh, it was.

John I wanted to be up there with you.

Robert *Did* you?

John Yes.

Robert Where?

John Up there.

Robert At the dinner table? (*Pause.*) You mean up there around the dinner table, or up upon the stage?

Pause.

John In the house.

Robert Around the dinner table?

John Yes.

Robert Oh, yes, that scene was heaven. (*Pause.*) It made me glad to be alive.

John It showed.

Robert The *audience* . . .

John Yes.

Robert That scene was a little play. It was a *poem* tonight.

John Yes.

Robert Just like a little *walnut*.

John Yes. (How do you mean?)

Robert *You* know . . .

John No.

Pause.

Robert Well, I mean that it was *meaty* . . .

John Yes . . .

Robert Uh, meaty on the *inside* . . .

John Yes?

Robert And tight all round.

John Ah.

Pause.

Robert Now *that* is superior theater.

John Yes. (*Pause.*) Mmm-hmm.

Robert Where did you say you were off to?

John Now?

Robert Yes.

John I was going for dinner.

Robert Ah.

John I've been feeling like a lobster.

Robert Ah.

John All day.

Robert Mmm. Shellfish.

John Yes.

Pause.

Robert I can't eat at night.

John No.

Robert No. My weight.

John You're having trouble with your weight?

Robert Yes, always. It's a constant fight.

John But you're trim enough.

Robert Do you think so?

John Yes.

Robert Then that makes it worthwhile. (*Pause.*) Thank you.

John Not at all. What are you up to this evening?

Robert Now, you mean?

John Yes.

Robert I thought I might go home and read.

John Ah.

Robert Perhaps take a walk.

John Ah.

Pause.

Robert Why'd you ask?

John No real reason.

Robert Oh.

John Just asked. I'm just asking.

Robert Well, *I* thought that I'd take a walk.

John Mmm.

Robert Why did you ask me that?

John No real reason at all. (*Pause.*) Unless you'd like to join me for a snack?

Robert A 'snack'. I really couldn't *eat* . . .

Pause.

John Well, then, some coffee. I could use the company.

Robert I'll walk with you a ways, then.

John Alright.

Robert Good.

Pause.

John You have some makeup on your face.

Robert Where?

John There. Behind your ear.

Robert Yes?

John Here. I'll get it. I'll get you some tissue.

Robert It's alright.

John No. Wait. We'll get it off.

John *goes after tissue;* **Robert** *stands on the stage. He does vocal exercises.*

Robert Did I get it on my coat?

John No. (*He moistens tissue with his saliva and rubs it on* **Robert**'*s face.*) There.

Robert Did we get it off?

John Yes.

Robert Good. I didn't get it on my coat?

John No.

Robert Good. Good. Thank you.

John Not at all.

Pause.

Robert Shall we go?

John Yes.

John *casually tosses the crumpled tissue toward the trash receptacle stage right. It misses the container and falls on the floor.*

Robert Mmm. One moment.

Robert *crosses right, picks up the tissue, and deposits it in the appropriate receptacle.*

Robert Alright. All gone. Let's go. (*Pause.*) Eh?

John Yes.

Robert I'm famished.

John Me too.

Robert Good.

They exit.

Scene 2

Robert *and* **John** *in the Wardrobe area.*

Robert Your hat.

Pause.

John Thank you.

Robert Like an oven in here.

John Yes.

Robert Got no space to *breathe*.

John No. (*Pause.*) Am I in your way?

Robert No. Not at all. (*Pause.*) Quite the contrary.

John (*handing* **Robert** *his hat*) Your hat.

Robert I thank you. (*Pause. Soliloquizing.*) My hat, my hat, my hat. (*Pause.*) Eh?

John *Mmm.*

Scene 3

Onstage. **John** *and* **Robert** *in the trenches, smoking the last fag.*

John They left him up there on the wire.

Robert Calm down.

John Those bastards.

Robert Yeah.

John My God. They stuck him on the wire and left him there for target practice.

Robert (*of cigarette*) Gimme that.

John Those dirty, dirty bastards.

Robert Yeah.

John My God.

Robert Calm down.

John *He* had a home; *he* had a family. (*Pause.*) Just like them. *He* thought that he was going home . . .

Robert Relax, we'll all be going home.

John On the last day, Johnnie, on the *last day* . . .

Robert That's the breaks, kid.

John Oh, my God, they're signin' it at noon. (*Pause.*) Poor Mahoney. Goes to raise the lousy flag, the Jerries cut him down like wheat . . . Johnnie, two more hours and we're going home. (*Pause.*) And those bastards went and cut him down.

Pause.

Robert That's the breaks.

John No. Not by me. Uh-*uh*. Not by a long shot.

Robert What are you doing?

John *gets up and peers over the trench.*

Robert What are you doing, Billy?

John *starts over the top.*

John You hear me, Heinies? Huh? This is for Richard J. Mahoney, Corporal AEF, from Dawson, Oklahoma. (*Pause.*) Do you hear me? It's not over yet. Not by a *long* shot. Do you hear me, Huns?

John *runs off right. A single shot is heard, then silence.* **Robert** *draws on his fag deeply, then stubs it out. He uncocks his rifle.*

Robert Well, looks like that's the end of it . . .

Scene 4

Robert *and* **John** *have just completed a curtain call for an Elizabethan piece.*

Robert Say, keep your point up, will you?

John When?

Robert When we're down left, eh, right before the head cut. You've been getting lower every night.

John I'm sorry.

Robert That's all right. Just make sure that you're never in line with my face. I'll show you: Look:

Robert *begins to demonstrate the fencing combination.*

You *parry* . . . *parry* . . . *THRUST*, but, see, you're thrusting high . . . aaaand *head cut.*
May we try it one more time?

John *nods.*

Robert Good.

They strike a pose and prepare to engage. They mime the routine as **Robert** *speaks lines.*

Robert And: 'But *fly* my *liege* and *think* no *more* of *me*.' Aaaaand *head cut.*

Eh? You're never in line with my face. We don't want any blood upon the stage.

Robert *knocks wood.*

John No.

Pause.

Robert Please knock on wood.

Pause.

John *knocks.*

Robert Good. Thank you.

Scene 5

Robert *and* **John** *are in a Dance Room.* **John** *is lounging, sweaty, after working out a bit.* **Robert** *is working at the barre.*

Robert Isn't it strange . . .

John Yes?

Robert That people will spend time and money on their face and body . . .

John Mmm?

Robert On smells, textures and appearances . . .

John Uh huh.

Robert And yet are content to sound like shopgirls and sheepherders.

John Ummm.

Pause.

Robert It's quite as important as physical beauty.

John On the stage, you mean.

Robert On the stage and otherwise.

John Mmm.

Robert *Sound.*

John Yes.

Robert The crown prince of phenomena.

John Quite.

Robert An ugly sound, to me, is more offensive than an ugly odor.

John Really?

Robert Yes. To me, an ugly *sound* is an extension of an ugly soul. An indice of lacking aesthetic. (*Pause.*) I don't like them. I don't like ugly sounds. I don't like the folks that make them. (*Pause.*) You think that's harsh, don't you?

John Not at all.

Robert You don't?

John No.

Robert I know. I'm strange about this. It's a peeve of mine. To me it's like an odor. Sound. For it emanates from within. (*Pause.*) Sound and odor germinate within, and are *perceived* within. (*Pause.*) You see?

John No.

Pause.

Robert All that I am saying is that it comes from within. (*Pause.*) Sound comes from within. You see?

John Mmmm.

Robert I am not opposed to odors. (*Pause.*) On principle.

John No.

Pause.

Robert Do you know when I was young my voice was very raspy.

John No.

Robert But I was vain, I was untaught. I felt my vocal quality – a defect, in effect – was a positive attribute, a contributory portion of my style.

John Mmm.

Robert What is style?

John What?

Robert Style is *nothing*.

John No?

Robert Style is a paper bag. Its only shape comes from its contents. (*Pause.*) However, I was young. I made a fetish of my imperfections.

John It's a common fault.

Robert It makes me blush today to think about it.

Pause.

John Don't think about it.

Pause.

Robert You're right. You start from the beginning and go through the middle and wind up at the end.

John Yes.

Pause.

Robert A little like a play. Keep your back straight.

John Mmm.

Robert We must not be afraid of process.

John No.

Robert We must not lie about our antecedents.

John No.

Robert We must not be second-class citizens. (*Pause.*) We must not be clowns whose sole desire is to please. We have a right to learn.

Pause.

John Is my back straight?

Robert No. (*Pause.*) Do you *follow* me?

John I think I do.

Robert We must not be afraid to *grow*. We must support each other, John. This is the wondrous thing *about* the Theater, this potential.

John Mmmm.

Robert Our history goes back as far as Man's. Our aspirations in the Theater are much the *same* as man's. (*Pause.*) (Don't you think?)

John Yes.

Pause.

Robert We *are* society. Keep your back straight, John. The mirror is your friend. (*Pause.*) For a few more years. (*Pause.*) What have we to fear, John, from *phenomena?* (*Pause.*) We are explorers of the *soul*.

Pause.

John Is my back straight?

Robert No.

Scene 6

The end of a day. **John** *is on the backstage telephone.*

John Oh, no. I can't. I'm going out with someone in the show. (*Pause.*) No, in fact, an *Actor*. (*Pause.*) I don't know . . . Midnight. (*Pause.*) I'd like that very much. (*Pause.*) Me, too. (*Pause.*) How have you been?

Robert *enters.*

Robert You ready?

John (*covering phone*) Yes. (*Into phone.*) I'll see you then. (*Pause.*) 'Bye.

He hangs up telephone.

Robert We all must have an outside life, John. This is an essential.

John Yes.

Robert Who was it?

Pause.

John A friend.

Scene 7

A short scene in which **John** *and* **Robert** *encounter each other coming into the theater for an early-morning rehearsal.*

Robert Good morning.

John Morning.

Robert 'Nother day, eh?

John Yes.

Robert Another day. (*He sighs.*) Another day.

Scene 8

Before a performance – at the makeup table.

John May I have the tissue, please? Thank you. How do you feel this evening?

Robert Tight. I feel a little tight. It's going to be a vibrant show tonight. I feel coiled up.

John Mmm.

Robert But I don't feel tense.

John No?

Robert No. Never feel tense. I almost never feel tense on stage. I feel ready to act. That's a lovely brush.

John This?

Robert No. The quarter-inch.

John This one?

Robert Yes. Is it new?

John It's an eighth-inch.

Robert That one?

John Yes.

Robert That's an eighth-inch?

John Yes.

Pause.

Robert Well, it's awfully splayed, don't you think?

John No.

Robert It's not splayed a bit?

John No.

Robert Well, it's not *new* . . . (Is it new?)

John No, I've had it a while.

Robert A while, eh?

John Yes.

Robert A long while?

John Yes.

Robert What is it, camel?

John It's sable.

Pause.

Robert (Sable brushes.) You keep your things well.

John Mmm.

Robert It's impressive. No. It's one of the things which impressed me first about you.

John Mmm.

Robert You take excellent care of your tools. (*Pause.*) May I ask you something, John?

John Of course.

Robert Could you do me a favor?

John What?

Pause.

Robert In our scene tonight . . .

John Yes?

Robert Mmmm . . .

John What?

Robert Could you . . . perhaps . . . *do* less?

John *Do* less?

Robert Yes.

John *Do* less???

Robert Yes . . .

Pause.

John Do less *what???*

Robert You know.

John You mean . . . what do you mean?

Pause.

Robert You know.

John Do you mean I'm walking on your scene? (*Pause.*) What do you mean?

Robert Nothing. It's a thought I had. An aesthetic consideration.

John Mmm.

Robert I thought maybe if you *did* less . . .

John Yes?

Robert *You* know.

John If I *did* less.

Robert Yes.

John Well, thank you for the thought.

Robert I don't think you have to be like that.

John I'm sorry.

Robert Are you?

John I accept the comment in the spirit in which it was, I am sure, intended.

Pause.

Robert It *was* intended in that spirit, John.

John I know it was.

Robert How could it be intended otherwise?

John It couldn't.

Robert Well, you *know* it couldn't.

John Yes, I know.

Robert It hurts me when you take it personally. (*He stands.*) Shit!

John What?

Robert My zipper's broken.

John Do you want a safety pin?

Robert I have one.

John (*rising, starting to leave*) Do you want me to send the woman in?

Robert No. No. I'll manage. Shit. Oh, shit.

John You're sure?

Robert Yes.

John You don't want the woman?

Robert No. I do not want the woman. Thank you.

John You want me to pin it for you?

Robert No.

John I'll do it. Let me pin it for you.

Robert No. Thank you. No. I'll get it.

John Oh, come on. I'll do it. Come on.

John *pulls out chair.*

Get up here. Come on. Get up.

Robert *gets up on the chair.*

John Give me the pin. Come on.

Robert *hands* **John** *the pin.* **John** *drops it on the floor.*

John Shit.

John *gets down on hands and knees to look for it.*

Robert Oh, Christ.

John You got another one?

Robert No. Oh, Christ, come on. Come on.

John I'm *looking* for it, for God's sake.

Robert There!

John Stand still now.

Robert Come on, come on.

John *attempts to pin* **Robert's** *fly.*

Robert Put it in.

John Just hold still for a moment.

Robert Come *on*, for God's sake!

John Alright. Alright. You know, I think you're gaining weight . . .

Robert Oh, fuck you. Will you stick it in?

John Hold still. There.

Robert Thank's a lot.

He gets off the chair.

John Good show!

Robert Thank you.

Scene 9

Onstage. A scene from a play in a lawyer's office. **Robert** *is behind a desk, talking on the telephone.*

Robert Perhaps you find it harsh, but I do not. I've always felt that we were friends. (*Pause.*) I know you have, and so have I.

John *enters the office.* **Robert** *motions him to sit.*

Robert I know you have. I feel that there is some common ground, I feel our interests are similar. (*Pause.*) No, not identical, but similar, certainly negotiable.

Robert *offers* **John** *a cigar from a humidor.* **John** *refuses.*

Robert (*pause*) I've always felt so. (*Pause.*) When? (*Pause.*) I'm sorry, I'm tied up the entire morning. (*Pause.*) Yes? (*Pause.*) Yes?

John *rises and walks over to look out the window.*

Robert Alright, then. (*Pause.*) And I'm sure this can be settled to our mutual satisfaction. (*Pause.*) So do I. I'll have my girl take care of it. (*Pause.*) Not at all. (*Pause.*) Not at all. (*Pause.*) And the very same to you. (*Pause.*) Goodbye. (*He hangs up the telephone. To* **John**.) Forgive me, David.

John Not at all. I've just been admiring the view.

Robert Lovely, isn't it?

John I should think one would get used to it.

Robert Well, it's been thirteen years, and I haven't seemed to do so.

John Yes. (*Pause.*) It's funny, you know, how things attain the force of habit . . .

Robert The force of habit . . . yes.

John Take me and Gillian.

Pause.

Robert Yes? (*Pause.*) Is that what you've come to talk about?
(*The intercom rings.* **Robert** *into intercom.*) Hold all calls, please. (*To* **John**.) Is there something wrong between you and Gillian?

John Gillian's going to have a baby.

Robert Why, this is marvelous. How long have you known?

John Since this morning.

Robert How marvelous!

John It isn't mine.

Robert It's not.

John No.

Robert Oh. (*Pause.*) I always supposed there was something one *said* in these situations . . . but I find . . . Do you know – that is, have you been told who the father is?

John Yes.

Robert Really. Who is it, David?

John It's you, John.

Robert Me!

John You.

Robert No.

John Yes.

Robert How preposterous.

John Is it?

Robert You know it is.

John Do I?

Robert Yes.

John Oh, John, John, John. (*Pause.*) I think that I'll have that cigar now.

Robert I think that I'll join you. (*Pause.*) She's told you that I am the husband.

Pause.

John No.

Pause.

Robert She's told you that I am the father.

John Yes. (*Pause.*) What are we going to do about this?

Robert I don't know, David. You could – I suppose you could do me some physical damage . . .

John Yes.

Robert Or we could sit and discuss this as gentlemen. Which would you prefer?

John Which, in the end, is more civilized, John?

Robert I don't know, David, I don't know. (*Long pause . . . intercom rings.*) I asked you to hold all calls. (*Pause.*) Perhaps *you* should take this.

Scene 10

Backstage in the Wardrobe area.

Robert The motherfucking leeches. The sots. (*Pause.*) The bloody boors. All of them . . . All of them . . .

John Who?

Robert All of them.

John All of whom?

Pause.

Robert What?

John All of whom?

Pause.

Robert You know. All of them. Bloody shits . . .

John What about them?

Robert Why can they not leave us alone? (*Pause.*) Eh?

John Yes.

Robert What? Eh?

John Yes.

Robert You're damn right. (*Sotto voce.*) Boring lunatics . . .

Scene 11

Onstage.

John Oh, the autumn.

Pause.

Robert Yes.

John Autumn weather.

Robert Yes.

John Oh, for the sun.

Robert Will you pass me my robe, please?

John Your laprobe.

Robert Yes. (*Business.*)

John Maman says just one more day, one more day, yet another week.

Robert Mmm.

John One more week.

Robert Would you please close the window?

John What? I'm sorry?

Robert Do you feel a draft?

John A slight draft, yes. (*Pause.*) Shall I close the window?

Robert Would you mind?

John No, not at all. (I love this window.) (*Pause. Closes the window.*)

Robert Thank you.

John Mmm.

Robert This room . . . this room.

John If we could leave this afternoon.

Robert Mmm?

John If we could just call . . . bring the carriage round, just leave this afternoon . . .

Robert It's much too cold . . .

John Just throw two shirts into a bag . . . a scarf . . .

Robert (. . . the roads . . .)

John Just meet the train. (*Pause.*) Venice . . .

Pause.

Robert It's much too cold.

Pause.

John Would you like a glass of tea?

Robert What? Thank you, yes.

John I like this room.

Robert Yes, so do I.

John I always have.

Pause.

Robert So have I.

John I'll ring for tea.

Pause.

Robert Thank you.

Scene 12

Backstage. **Robert** *and* **John** *changing clothes.*

Robert I wish they'd wash this stuff more often.

John Mmm.

Robert Smells like a gym in here.

John The building's old.

Robert Yes. Yes. (*Pause.*) Tired?

John No. A little.

Robert Mmm.

Scene 13

John *and* **Robert** *are sitting and reading a new script.*

Robert Good. Alright. Got a match?

John *lights* **Robert's** *cigarette.*

Robert Mmm. Thank you.

John Mmm.

Robert Alright. Good. (*Starts reading.*) 'One day blends into the next' . . . I'm not going to do the accent. Eh?

John Yes.

Robert Good. One day blends into the next. Scorching sun . . . shiv'ring moon. Salt . . . saltwater . . .

John 'It'll rain soon' . . . I'm   **Robert** (*musing*) Salt . . .
sorry?   saltwater . . .

Robert Eh?

John I'm sorry. What?

Robert No, I'm just thinking. Salt. Saltwater. Eh? The thought. He lets you see the thought there.

Pause.

John Mmm.

Pause.

Robert Salt! Sweat. His life flows out. (*Pause.*) Then salt*water!* Eh?

John Yes.

Robert To the *sea.*

John Yes.

Robert Alright. Good.

They go back.

Robert 'One day blends into the next. Salt. Saltwater.'

John 'It'll rain soon.'

Robert 'Rain? What do *you* know about it?' (*Pause.*) 'I've spent my whole life on the sea, and all that I know is the length of my ignorance. Which is *complete*, sonny.' (*Pause.*) 'My ignorance is complete.'

John 'It's gotta rain.'

Robert The motif, eh, the leitmotif. He takes the descant through the scene – 'It's got to rain.' You look at it, he does the same thing through the play.

Pause.

John Mmm.

Robert Go on.

Pause.

John 'It's gotta rain.'

Robert 'Tell it to the marines.'

John 'It doesn't rain, I'm going off my nut.'

Robert You see: it *will* rain, it's *got* to rain, it *doesn't* rain . . . alright, alright. 'Just take it easy, kid . . . what you don't want to do now is sweat.' (*Pause.*) 'Believe me.'

Pause.

John 'We're never getting out of this alive.' (*Pause.*) 'Are we?'

Robert 'How do you want it?'

John 'Give it to me straight.'

Pause.

Robert 'Kid, we haven't got a chance in hell.' (*Pause. Musing.*) 'We haven't got a chance in hell. We're never getting out of this alive.' (*Pause.*) Eh? He sets it on the sea, we are marooned, he tells us that the sea is life, and then we're never getting out of it alive. (*Pause.*) Eh?

Pause.

John Yes.

Robert The man could write . . . Alright. Alright. (*Pause.*) Let's go back a bit.

Pause.

John (*sighs*) 'It'll rain soon . . .'

Scene 14

Robert *and* **John** *are eating Chinese food at the makeup table between shows.*

Robert You had an audition this afternoon, eh?

John Yes.

Robert How did it go?

John Well, I thought.

Robert Yes?

Pause.

John They were receptive. I thought it went well.

Robert How did you feel?

John I felt good; they liked it.

Robert That's nice.

John I thought so.

Robert That's very nice. (*Pause. Eating.*) There are two classes of phenomena.

John There are.

Pause.

Robert There are those things we *can* control and those things which we cannot.

John Mmm.

Robert You can't control what someone thinks of you.

John No.

Robert That is up to them. They may be glum, they may be out-of-sorts. Perhaps they are neurotic.

John How's your duck?

Robert Fine. (*Pause.*) One *can* control, however, one's actions. One's intentions.

John Pass the bread, please.

Robert That is all one can control.

John Please pass the bread.

Robert You're eating bread?

John Yes.

Robert Oh. (*Pause.*) Here it is.

John Thanks.

Robert If they hadn't liked you, that would not have signified that you weren't a good actor.

John No. I think I know that.

Robert Yes. I think perhaps you do. (*Pause.*) Yes. I'm glad they liked you, though.

John Thank you.

Robert You think they're going to hire you?

John I don't know.

Robert Well, I hope they do.

John I hope so, too.

Robert That would be nice for you.

John Yes.

Pause.

Robert (*to self*) Good things for good folk.

Scene 15

John *and* **Robert** *are dressing backstage.*

Robert We should do this whole frigging thing in rehearsal clothes, you know? Eh? Do it in blue jeans and T-shirts and give it some life, you know?

John Yes.

Robert Eh? And give it some *guts*. (*Pause.*) Give *guts* to it. (*Pause.*) And to hell with experimentation. Artistic experimentation is shit. Huh?

John Right.

Robert You're frigging well told. (*Pause.*) Two *actors*, some *lines* . . . and an audience. That's what I say. Fuck 'em all.

Scene 16

Onstage. The Barricades.

Robert And the people cry for truth; the people cry for freedom from the vicious lies and slanders of the ages . . . the slanders of the body and the soul. The heart cries out: the memory says man has always lived in chains . . . has always lived in chains . . . (*Pause.*) Bread, bread, bread, the people scream . . . we drown their screaming with our heads in cups, in books . . . in newspapers . . . between the breasts of women . . . in our work . . . enough. A new day rises . . . those who must connect themselves to yesterday for succor will be left behind . . . their souls are in the histories, their heads on pikes around the buildings of our government. Now we must look ahead . . . Our heads between the breasts of women, plight our troth to that security far greater than protection of mere rank or fortune. Now: we must dedicate ourselves to spirit: to the spirit of humanity; to life. (*Pause.*) To the barricades! (*Pause.*) Bread, bread, bread.

Scene 17

At the makeup table.

Robert A makeup table. Artificial light. The scent of powder. Tools. Sticks. Brushes. Tissues. (*Pause.*) Cold *cream.* (*Pause.*) Greasepaint. (*Pause.*) Greasepaint! What is it? Some cream base, some coloring . . . texture, smell, color . . . analyze it and what have you? Meaningless component parts, though one could likely say the same for anything . . . *But* mix and package it, affix a label, set it on a makeup table . . . a brush or two . . .

John Would you please shut up?

Pause.

Robert Am I disturbing you?

John You are.

Pause.

Robert Enough to justify this breach of etiquette?

John What breach? What etiquette?

Robert John . . .

John Yes?

Robert When one's been in the Theater as long as I . . .

John Can we do this later?

Robert I feel that there is something here of worth to you.

John You do?

Robert Yes.

John (*sighs*) Let us hear it then.

Robert Alright. You know your attitude, John, is not of the best. It isn't. It just isn't.

John (*pause*) It isn't?

Robert Forms. The Theater's a closed society. Constantly abutting thoughts, the feelings, the emotions of our colleagues. Sensibilities, (*Pause.*) bodies . . . *forms* evolve. An etiquette, eh? In our personal relations with each other. Eh, John? In our personal relationship.

Pause.

John Mmm.

Robert One generation sows the seeds. It instructs the preceding . . . that is to say, the *following* generation . . . from the quality of its actions. Not from its discourse, John, no, but organically. (*Pause.*) You can learn a lot from keeping your mouth shut.

John You can.

Robert Yes. And perhaps this is not the place to speak of attitudes.

John Before we go on.

Robert Yes. But what is 'life on stage' but attitudes?

John (*pause*) What?

Robert Damn little.

Pause.

John May I use your brush?

Robert Yes. (*Hands* **John** *brush.*) One must speak of these things, John, or we will go the way of all society.

John Which is what?

Robert Take too much for granted, fall away and die.
(*Pause.*) On the boards, or in society at large. There must be
law, there must be a reason, there must be tradition.

Pause.

John I'm sorry that I told you to shut up.

Robert No, you can't buy me off that cheaply.

John No?

Robert No.

Pause.

John Would you pass me the cream, please?

Robert Certainly. (*Passes the cream.*) Here is the cream.

John Thank you.

Scene 18

Onstage. The famous lifeboat scene.

Robert One day blends into the next. Scorching sun,
shivering moon. Salt. Saltwater . . .

John It'll rain soon.

Robert Rain . . . ? What do *you* know about it? (*Pause.*) I've
spent my whole life on the sea, and all that I know is the
length of my ignorance. Which is *complete*, sonny. (*Pause.*) My
Ignorance is complete.

John It's gotta rain.

Robert Tell it to the marines.

John It doesn't rain, I'm going off my nut.

Robert Just take it easy, kid . . . What you don't wanna do
now is sweat. (*Pause.*) Believe me.

Pause.

John We're never getting out of this alive. (*Pause.*) Are we?

Robert How do you want it?

John Give it to me straight.

Robert Kid, we haven't got a chance in hell. (*Pause.*) But you know what? (*Pause.*) You shouldn't let it get you down. And you know why? 'Cause that's the gamble. That's what life on the sea is about.

John Can I tell you something?

Robert Shoot.

John You're full of it, I mean it. Don't you tell me about Men and the Sea, because that's been out of the picture for years. If it ever existed. No, it probably did. Back in the days when a man had a stake in what he went out after, when he had a stake in his ship . . . and a stake in himself . . . But *now* . . . Now we're dyin' 'cause some black bastard shipowner in Newport decided that rather than make his ships safe for men, it was cheaper to overinsure them. (*Pause.*) *THAT'S* what we're dying for . . .

Pause. The Kid breaks down.

Robert Danny . . . Danny . . . A ship!!! *A SHIP!!!*

Scene 19

John *and* **Robert** *are standing in the wings.* **John** *is about to go on.*

Robert Ephemeris, ephemeris, eh?

John What?

Robert Ephemeris, ephemeris.

Pause.

John What are you saying?

Robert Time passes.

Pause.

John What comes after: 'The men got together, ma'am, and we kind of thought you'd like to have this'?

Robert She says, 'Thank you.'

John I'm aware of that, I think. *After* that. What comes after that?

Robert Your line?

John Yes.

Robert Uh . . .

John Have you got a script?

Robert What would I be doing with a script?

John I'm going to go get a script.

Robert Wait. I know what the line is . . .

John What?

Robert Uh, after you give her the watch, right?

John Yes.

Robert Right. You give her the *watch*. You give her the *watch* . . .

John And?

Robert Ah, Christ . . . you hand the cunt the watch: 'Ma'am, we kinda thought that maybe . . .'

John 'The men all got together, ma'am . . .'

Robert Yes. And . . . um . . . this is ridiculous . . . You give her the *watch* . . . (What's *her* line?)

John 'Thank you.'

Pause.

Robert Ah, fuck. You'd better get a script. You want me to?

John Sshhhhh!

Pause.

Robert What?

John Shut up. I'm trying to hear my cue.

Pause.

Robert What's happening?

Pause.

John I think I missed my cue. (*Pause.*) I think I missed my cue.

Pause.

Robert What's happening?

John Sshhhhhhh!

Robert Can you see?

John I'm going on. (*Pause.*) I'm going to go on. (*Pause.*) What do you think?

Robert *shrugs. Pause.*

John Christ. I'm going out . . .

Robert You want me to get a script?

John I've missed my cue . . . I've missed my cue . . .

Robert Well, go out there . . . go on.

Pause.

John Oh, God. I've missed my cue . . .

Robert Get *out* there . . .

John (*making his entrance*) 'Missus Wilcox??? Missus Wilcox, ma'am? The men all got together . . .'

Scene 20

Backstage. **John** *is dressing.* **Robert** *enters, speaking slowly to himself.*

Robert   Oh God, oh God, oh God, oh God, oh God. (*He sees* **John**. *Pause.*) New sweater?

John   Yes.

Robert   Nice.

John   Mmm.

Robert   What is it?

John   What?

Robert   What is it? Cashmere?

John   I don't know.

Robert   Looks good on you.

John   Thanks.

Robert   Mmm.

Scene 21

Backstage. **John** *is at the telephone, waiting.* **Robert** *enters.*

Robert   And everybody wants a piece. They all have got to get a piece.

John   (*into phone*)   I'll wait.

Robert   We spend our adult lives bending over for incompetents. For ten-percenters, sweetheart unions, everybody in the same bed together. Agents. All the bloodsuckers. The robbers of the cenotaph. Who are we?

John   Who? (*Into phone.*) Hello?

Robert   Who indeed?

John   I'm holding for Miss Erenstein.

Robert   If we cannot speak to each other . . . what do we have but our fellow workers? If we do not have that, what do we have? Who can speak our language, eh?

John   (*to* **Robert**)   And what of talent?

Robert And what of it? (*Pause.*) What of humanity?

Pause.

John What?

Robert I don't know. (*Pause.*) Let's get a drink.

John I'm on the phone.

Robert Hang it up.

John (*into phone*) Hello, Bonnie? *John.* How *are* you . . . ?

Robert We enslave ourselves.

John (*into phone*) *No!*

Robert (God).

John (*into phone*) Why, *thank* you. Thank you very much. (*Pause.*) On the *film* . . . ? Yes? Yes? I'll check my book.

Robert One does not have to check one's 'book' to get a *drink*. (*To himself.*) A drink cannot buy *itself.*

John (*covering phone*) Do you know who this *is*?

Robert I am going to drink. For I must drink now. Do you know why?

John Why?

Pause.

Robert It is fitting. (*Exits.*)

John (*into phone*) Yes. Eleven's *fine*. (*Pause.*) *W*onderful.

Scene 22

Backstage. **Robert** and **John** *are taking off their makeup.*

Robert Fucking leeches.

John Mmm. Pass me the tissue, please?

Robert They'll praise you for the things you never did and pan you for a split second of godliness. What do they know?

They create nothing. They come in the front door. They don't even buy a ticket.

John No.

Robert They've praised you too much. I do not mean to detract from your reviews – you deserve praise, John, much praise.

John Thank you.

Robert Not, however, for those things which they have praised you for.

John In your opinion.

Robert Yes, John, yes. From now on. (*Pause.*) You must be very careful who you listen to. From whom you take advice.

John Yes.

Robert Never take *advice* . . .

John Yes . . .

Robert . . . from *people* . . .

John May I have my comb, please?

Robert . . . who do not have a vested interest, John, in your eventual success.

John I won't.

Robert Or, barring that, in Beauty in the Theater.

John I thought that they were rather to the point.

Robert You did.

John Yes.

Robert Your reviews.

John Yes.

Robert All false modesty aside.

John Yes.

Robert Oh, the Young, the Young, the Young, the Young.

John The Farmer in the Dell.

Robert Oh, I see.

John Would you hand me my scarf, please?

Pause.

Robert You fucking TWIT.

John I beg your pardon?

Robert I think that you heard me. (*Takes towel from **John**'s area and begins to use it.*)

Pause.

John Robert.

Robert What?

John Use your own towels from now on.

Robert They're at the laundry.

John Get them back.

Scene 23

*A dark stage, one worklight lit. **John** is rehearsing.*

John
Now all the youth of England are on fire
And silken dalliance in the wardrobe lies.
Now thrive the Armourers and honour's thought
Reigns solely in the breast of every man.

Robert (*offstage*) Ah, sweet poison of the actor, rehearsing in an empty theater upon an empty stage . . .

John Good evening.

Robert . . . but full of life, full of action, full of resolve, full of youth. (*Pause.*) Please continue. (*Pause.*) Please, please continue. I'd like you to . . . I'm sorry. Does this upset you? Does it upset you that someone is watching? I'm sorry, I can understand that. (*Pause.*) It's good. It's *quite* good. I was watching you for a while. I hope you don't mind. Do you mind?

John I've only been here a minute or so.

Robert And I've watched you all that time. It seemed so long. It was so full. You're very good, John. Have I told you that lately? You are becoming a very fine actor. The flaws of youth are the perquisite of the young. It is the perquisite of the young to possess the flaws of youth.

John It's fitting, yes . . .

Robert Ah, don't mock me, John. You shouldn't mock me. It's too easy. It's not good for you, no. And that is a lesson which we have to learn. (*Pause.*) Which you have to learn.

John And what is that?

Robert That it is a hurtful fault, John, to confuse sincerity with weakness. (*Pause.*) And I must tell you something.

John Yes.

Robert About the Theater – and this is a wondrous thing about the Theater – and John, one of the ways in which it's most like life . . .

John And what is that?

Pause.

Robert Simply this. That in the *Theater* (as in life – and the Theater is, of course, a *part* of life . . . No?) . . . Do you see what I'm saying? I'm saying, as in a grocery store, that you cannot separate the *time* one spends . . . that is, it's all part of one's *life*. (*Pause.*) In addition to the fact that what's happening on *stage* is life . . . of a sort . . . I mean, it's part of your *life*. (*Pause.*) Which is one reason I'm so *gratified* (if I may presume, and I recognize that it may be a presumption) to see you . . . to see the *young* of the Theater . . . (And it's *not* unlike one's children) . . . following in the footpaths of . . . following in the footsteps of . . . those who have gone before. (*Pause.*) Do you see what I am saying? I would like to think you *did*. Do you? John? (*Pause.*) Well . . . well. Goodnight, John.

Pause.

John　Goodnight.

Robert　*Good*night. I'll see you.

He waves, starts to exit.

John　*Good* night. (*Long pause.*)

John *examines the wings where* **Robert** *has exited.* **John** *takes the stage.*

They sell the pasture now to buy the horse
Following the mirror of all Christian Kings
With the winged heels as English Mercuries.

Pause.

For now sits Expectation in the air.

Pause.

And hides a sword.

Pause. He talks into the wings.

Are you back in there? Robert? Are you back in there? (*Pause.*) I *see* you in there. I see you there, Robert.

Robert　(*offstage voice*)　I'm just leaving.

John　You were not just leaving, you were . . . *looking* at me.

Robert　On my way *out*, John. On my way *out*. Christ, but you make me feel small. You make me feel *small*, John. I don't feel good.

Pause.

John　Are you crying? Are you crying, Robert, for chrissakes? (*Pause.*) *Christ.* Are you crying?

Robert　Yes.

Pause.

John　Well, stop *crying*.

Robert Yes. I will.

John No, stop it *now*. Stop it. Please.

Pause. **Robert** *stops crying.*

Robert Better?

Pause.

John Yes. (*Pause.*) Are you alright?

Robert Oh, yes. I'm alright. I'm fine. Thank you, John. (*Pause.*) Well, I suppose I'll . . . (You're going to work summore, eh?)

John Yes.

Robert Then I suppose I'll . . . (Well, I was leaving *anyway*.) (*Pause.*) Goodnight. Goodnight, John.

Pause.

John Are you alright now? (*Raising his voice.*) Robert! Are you alright now?

Robert (*far offstage*) Yes. Thank you. Yes. I'm alright now.

Pause.

John *takes the stage again, is about to begin declaiming.*

Robert (*from far offstage*) You're not angry with me, are you?

John No.

Robert You're sure?

John Yes.

Pause.

Robert I'm glad, John. (*Pause.*) Thank you.

John Goodnight, Robert. (*Pause.*) Robert? (*Pause.*)

John *takes the stage.*

Now all the Youth of England are on fire . . .

Pause.

Robert?

Pause.

Robert Yes, John?

John Are you out there?

Robert Yes, John.

John (*sotto voce*) Shit.

Scene 24

Onstage. **Robert** *and* **John** *are dressed in surgical smocks, and stand behind a form on an operating table.*

Robert Give me some suction there, doctor, will you . . . that's good.

John Christ, what I wouldn't give for a cigarette.

Robert Waaal, just a few more minutes and I think I'll join you in one. (*Pause.*) Nervous, Jimmy?

John No. Yes.

Robert No need to be. A few years, you'll be doing these in your sleep. Suction. Retractor. (*Business.*) No, the *large* retractor.

John Sorry.

Robert It's alright. Give me another one, will you?

Business.

John (*pointing*) What's that?

Pause. **Robert** *shakes his head minutely.* **John** *nods his head.*

John What's that?

Robert *minutely but emphatically shakes his head.*

Pause.

John *mumbles something to* **Robert.** **Robert** *mumbles something to* **John.**

Pause.

Robert Would you, uh, can you give me some sort of reading on the, uh, electro . . . um . . . on the . . . Would you get me one, please? (*Motioning* **John** *offstage.*) No . . . on the, uh . . . would you get me a reading on this man?

John (*pointing*) What's *that!!!?*

Robert What is what? Eh?

John What's that near his spleen? (*Pause.*) A curious growth near his spleen?

Robert What?

John A Curious Growth Near His Spleen? (*Pause.*) Is that one, there?

Robert No, I think not. I think you cannot see a growth near his spleen for some *time* yet. So would you (as this man's in shock) . . . would you get me, please, give me a reading on his vital statements. Uh, *Functions* . . . ? Would you do that one thing for me, please?

John (*sotto voce*) We've done that one, Robert.

Robert I fear I must disagree with you, Doctor. Would you give me a reading on his vital *things*, if you please? Would you? (*Pause.*) For the love of God?

John (*sotto voce*) That's in the other part.

Robert No, it is *not*. He's in shock. He's in shock, and I'm becoming miffed with you. Now: if you desire to work in this business again, will you give me a reading? If you wish to continue here inside the hospital? (*Pause.*) Must I call a *policeman!!?* (*Pause.*) Have you no feeling? The man's in deepest shock!!!

Pause. **John** *takes off his mask and walks away.*

Robert And now where are you going? (*Pause.*) You *quitter!!*

Another pause.

(*To audience.*) Ladies and gentlemen. What we have seen here today is – I won't say a 'perfect' – but a very good example of successful surgical technique, performed under modern optimum conditions, uh . . . and with a minimum of *fuss* . . . a minimum of *mess* and *bother* . . . and I hope that you have . . . (*The curtain is being rung down on him.*) . . . that you have found it every bit . . .

Curtain is down. Hold.

Robert (*generally*) Does anybody have a script?

Scene 25

Backstage. **Robert** *appears, holding his left wrist with his right hand.*

Robert Oh God, oh God, I've cut myself.

John (*entering*) What have you done?

Robert I'm bleeding. Oh, my God . . .

John Christ.

Robert What a silly accident. Can you believe this?

John Come on.

Robert Where?

John We're going to the hospital.

Robert Oh, no. Oh, no. I'm alright, really.

John Come on.

Robert No. What would they say? Kidding aside. (*Pause.*) No. I'm quite alright. My razor slipped and now I'm fine. I had a moment, though. I did. (*Pause.*) John . . . (*Pause.*) John . . .

John Yes.

Robert Did you know in olden times they used to say 'clean-shaven like an actor'? (*Pause.*) Did you know that?

John Are you alright?

Robert Oh, yes. I'm fine. I've lost a little blood is all. It's nothing, really. (*Pause.*) A mishap. (*Pause.*) Clean-shaven . . .

John God, what's wrong with you?

Robert There's nothing wrong with me. My hand slipped. (*Pause.*) I'm tired. That's all. I'm tired. (*Pause.*) I need to rest. We all need rest. We all need rest. It's much too much. It's just too much. I'm tired. (*Pause.*) You understand? I'm *tired*.

John Well, I'm calling you a doctor.

Robert No. You're not. No. Please. I'm only tired. I'm going to go home. I'm only tired. We think we see things clearly when we haven't enough sleep. But we do not. I've cut myself. I've dirtied up the basin. (*Pause.*) I'm going to go home now.

John I'll come home with you.

Robert No. Thank you. I'll get home alone. I only have to rest now. Thank you. (*Pause.*) But thank you all the same.

John I'll take you home.

Robert What? No. I think I'm only going to sit here for a moment. (*Pause.*) I'll be alright. I'll be alright tomorrow. I'll be my old self. I'm alright *now*. (*Smiles. Pause.*) I'm only going to rest a moment . . . and then I'll go home.

John *looks to* **Robert** *for a moment, then exits.* **Robert** *remains onstage alone for a moment, then slowly exits.*

Scene 26

Backstage, after a show.

Robert I loved the staircase scene tonight.

John You did?

Robert Just like a poem.

Pause.

John I thought the execution scene worked beautifully.

Robert No. You *didn't*.

John Yes. I did.

Pause.

Robert *Thank* you. Getting cold, eh?

John Yes.

Robert (*to himself*) It's getting cold. (*Aloud.*) You know, my father always wanted me to be an actor.

John Yes?

Robert Always wanted me to be . . .

Pause.

John Well! (*Crosses and picks up umbrella.*)

Robert It's raining?

John I think it will. You got a fag?

Robert Yes. Always wanted me to be.

Robert *hands* **John** *a cigarette.*

John Thank you.

Robert Mmm.

John Got a match?

Robert You going out?

John Yes.

Robert Where? A party?

John No. I'm going with some people.

Robert Ah.

John You have a match?

Robert No.

John *hunts for a match on the makeup table.*

John Are you going out tonight?

Robert I don't know; I suppose so.

John Mmm.

Robert I'm not eating too well these days.

John No, eh?

Robert No.

John Why?

Robert Not hungry.

John *picks up matchbook, struggles to light match.*

Robert I'll get it.

John Do you mind?

Robert No.

Robert *takes matchbook and lights* **John**'s *cigarette.*

John Thank you.

Pause.

Robert A life spent in the Theater.

John Mmm.

Robert Backstage.

John Yes.

Robert The bars, the house, the drafty halls. The penciled scripts . . .

John Yes.

Robert Stories. Ah, the stories that you hear.

John I know.

Robert It all goes so fast. It goes so quickly.

Long pause.

John You think that I might borrow twenty 'til tomorrow?

Robert What, you're short on cash?

John Yes.

Robert Oh. Oh. (*Pause.*) Of course. (*He digs in his pocket. Finds money and hands it to* **John**.)

John You're sure you won't need it?

Robert No. No, not at all. No. If I don't know how it is, who does?

Pause.

John Thank you.

Robert Mmm. Goodnight.

John Goodnight.

Robert You have a nice night.

John I will.

Robert Goodnight.

John *exits. Pause.*

Robert Ephemeris, ephemeris. (*Pause.*) 'An actor's life for me.'

Robert *composes himself and addresses the empty house. He raises his hand to stop imaginary applause.*

You've been so kind . . . Thank you, you've really been so kind. You know, and I speak, I am sure, not for myself alone, but on behalf of all of us . . . (*Composes himself.*) . . . All of us here, when I say that these . . . *these* moments make it all . . . they make it all worthwhile.

Pause. **John** *quietly reappears.*

Robert You know . . .

Robert *sees* **John**.

John They're locking up. They'd like us all to leave.

Robert I was just leaving.

John Yes, I know, (*Pause.*) I'll tell them.

Robert Would you?

John Yes.

Pause.

Robert Thank you.

John Goodnight.

Robert Goodnight.

Pause.

John *exits*.

Robert (*to himself*) The lights dim. Each to his own home. Goodnight. Goodnight. Goodnight.

The Woods

The Characters:
Ruth
Nick

Scenes:
1 Dusk
2 Night
3 Morning

Setting:

The porch of a summer house, early September

The Woods was first produced by the St Nicholas Theater
Company, Chicago, Illinois, 11 November 1977, with the
following cast:

Ruth	Patti LuPone
Nick	Peter Weller

Directed by David Mamet
Set by Michael Merritt
Lighting by Robert Christen
Graphic design by Lois Grimm

Presented in arrangement with Ken Marsolais

Scene 1

Dusk

Ruth *and* **Nick** *are sitting on the porch.*

Ruth These seagulls they were up there, one of them was up there by himself.
He didn't want the other ones.
They came, he'd flap and get them off.
He left this one guy stay up there a minute.

Nick Tell me.

Ruth They flew off.

Pause.

Nick We have a lot of them. And herons.

Ruth You have herons?

Nick Yes. I think. I haven't seen them in a while.
We did when I was young.

Ruth Do they stay in the winter, too?

Nick No.

Ruth (*to self*) No.
We'll need more blankets soon.

Nick Were you cold last night?

Ruth I think you were dreaming. Yes. A little.
You took all the blankets. Were you dreaming?

Nick Yes.

Ruth I thought so. I hunched over next to you.
I held you.
Could you feel that?

Nick Yes.

Ruth I went down for a walk.

Nick Where?

Ruth Down by the Lake. All around.
I sat down and I listened, you know?
To the laps.
Time passed.

Pause.

I threw these stones.
I picked this stick up and I drew with it.

Nick What did you draw?

Ruth All sorts of things.

Nick What?

Ruth Patterns.

Pause.

The fish jumped. Everything smelled like iodine.

Nick Mmmm.

Ruth You could live up here. Why not?

Pause.

People could.
You could live right out in the country.
I slept so good yesterday.
All the crickets. You know?
With the rhythm.
You wait.
And you hear it.
Chirp.
Chirp chirp.
Not 'chirping'.

Pause.

Not '*chirping*', really.

Birds chirp.
Birds chirp, don't they, Nick?
Birds?

Nick Crickets, too, I think.

Ruth Yes?

Nick (*to self*) 'I heard crickets chirp.'
'The crickets chirped.'
(*Aloud.*) Yes.

Ruth I thought so. What do frogs do?

Nick They croak.

Pause.

Ruth I listened. All night long. They get soft at dawn.
Maybe they go to sleep.
Maybe the sun makes the air different and they become
harder to hear. I don't know.

Pause.

Who knows what's happening?
Down by the Lake there is a rotten boat.
A big green rowboat.
It might be from here to here.
It's rotten and the back is gone, but I'll bet it was pretty big.
I sat in it.
Inside the front was pointed up. It smelled real dry.
I mooshed around and this is how it sounded on the sand.
Swssshh. Chhhrssssh. Swwwssshhhh.
Very dry.
You know. I think I would of liked to go to sea.
Girls couldn't go to sea.
As cabin boys or something . . .

Nick They had woman pirates.

Ruth They were outlaws. Men would not let women go to
sea.

Nick The Vikings.

Ruth They let women go?

Nick Sure.

Ruth No. No. I don't think so.

Nick No?

Ruth Uh-uh. I heard of Vikings. Viking Women.
They would stay home and make clothes.
They used to bash the babies' heads in.
All the little girls.
They'd kill them. Did you know that, Nicky?

Nick Yes.

Ruth At birth?

Nick Yes.

Pause.

Ruth You heard that?

Nick Yes. I read it.

Pause.

Ruth Not all of them.
A lot of them.
The Vikings.

Pause.

Poor babes.
What do you think of that?

Nick Give me a kiss. (*She goes to him. They kiss.*)

Ruth I like it here.

Pause.

Can you smell the iodine?

Nick Yes.

Ruth Ozone. Can you smell it? Can you smell ozone?

Nick Now?

Ruth No. I mean, does ozone smell?
The thing itself?

Nick I think so.

Pause.

Ruth They told us after the storms the ozone came from electricity.

Nick (*to self*) . . . electrical discharges.

Ruth But now we have Ozone Alerts, they tell you it's no good for you.
Who *knows* what's good for you?
The Vikings had these lovely Northern Women and they used to bash their heads in.

Pause.

Oh, well.
Oh, well.
Who *knows* what's good for them?

Pause.

If this was mine, I'd come here all the time.
I think it's wild here, Nick.
I saw a raccoon.

Nick When?

Ruth Last night. On my walk.

Nick You should have woke me up.

Ruth You were asleep.

Nick I would have gone with you.

Ruth No. You were dreaming. And then when I saw it I was far from here. I heard a noise, I turned around, and there was this raccoon.

Nick Where?

Ruth Over there. I saw his eyes. He ran off.

Nick They get in the garbage.

Ruth No. I know. They eat it. When I saw it, I did not know what it was. Then it ran off.

Pause.

Nick We had them up here all the time.

Ruth When you were young.

Nick We'd catch them in a milk container.

Ruth Are they vicious?

Nick Very.

Ruth Yes. I thought so.

Nick And you couldn't keep them 'cause they'd gnaw their way out.

Ruth I was thinking . . . wait. Wait! They ate wood? The raccoons?

Nick No. You know. They'd chew it.

Nick To get *out*.

Nick Yes.

Pause.

Ruth Yes. I was thinking.

Nick Tell me.

Ruth Things that people like.
I thought the things that people like – I should have woke you up 'cause I was thinking on my walk – I thought our *appetites* are just the body's way to tell us things that we may need.

Pause.

Nick (*looking at Lake*) Fishes.

Ruth Where are they?

Nick Down there.

Pause.

Ruth What do you think? Our appetites.

Nick Say it again.

Ruth The liking that we have for things – desire – is just our body's way to tell us things.

Pause.

When we see someone – some woman on the beach – we say that she is beautiful.

Pause.

That's because perhaps of what is in her.
Small breasts. (*Pause.*) Maybe large.
The way she holds her back.
We see her and we know if we would breed with her, the things that would come out of it improve the race.
What do you think about that? Appetites.

Nick What about food?

Pause.

Ruth What about it?

Nick Tastes we have for it.

Ruth (*pause*) Tastes.

Nick Yes.

Ruth The tastes we have for it.

Nick Yes.

Ruth Food.

Pause.

Are you hungry?

Nick No.

Pause.

Ruth It must be the same.
Our body says we need these things.
They all come from the ground.
The vegetables.

Pause.

Minerals.
All pills and ointments.
Everything comes from the ground, in some way or another.
Then we eat it.
Medicine . . . I've thought about this . . .
What they give us are just things that come out of the
ground.
Or that we make. If they are concentrated, or we alter them,
so we can swallow them.
All things come from the ground.

Pause.

And the way that they found out was folks would eat them.
We would keep the good and we would pass the bad things
off.
I saw the fish grab insects right out of the air.
It all has properties. It all is only things the way they are.

Pause.

That is all there ever was.

Pause.

What they are and what they do.
And that is beauty.

Pause.

Nick What about cigarettes?

Pause.

Ruth Cigarettes?

Nick Yes.

Ruth They are bad for you.

Nick I know.

Ruth Why do we smoke them?

Nick Yes.

Ruth (*sigh*) We fall away from ourselves. We grow fat. We fall away. The women, too. And men. We pick the people that we know are bad for us. We do that all the time.

Nick We do. (*Pause.*) Why?

Ruth I don't know. Nothing lasts. (*Pause.*) This is what I thought down on the rowboat. It had rotted.
It had gone back to the Earth. We all go.
That is why the Earth is good for us.
When we look for things that don't go back, we become sick.

Pause.

That is when we hurt each other.
I thought about you and me.

Nick You did.

Ruth Down on the rowboat, yes.

Nick What did you think, Ruth?

Ruth Coming up here. How you asked me.
So little counts. Nick.
Just the things we do.

Pause.

To each other. The right things.

Pause.

That's what I think. (*Pause.*)
The frog *croaks?*

Nick Come here.

Ruth Does it?

Nick Yes. Come here. (*She does so. They kiss.*)

Ruth Are you happy now?

Nick Yes.

Ruth And she said they had a bear here.

Nick Who said that?

Ruth The woman.

Nick When?

Ruth Her mother saw one. Long ago.

Nick *Here?*

Ruth Right here.

Nick When?

Ruth When she was young.

Nick A wild bear.

Ruth Yes. She told me they had built the house upon its cave, and it came back.
It used to keep on coming here.
And then it went away, and this is when she saw it, it came back – her mother said – when it was going to die. Just like in Russia.

Pause.

To get beneath the house.

Nick When was this?

Ruth Long ago.

Nick A wild bear.

Ruth Yes. A long, long time ago.

Nick He'd be long dead now.

Ruth *Long* dead.

Nick They still have them up *there.*

Ruth Where?

Nick In Canada.

Ruth Bears.

Nick Not around here.

Ruth No.

Nick Up where it's wild.

Ruth They have a lot of land.

Nick Down, maybe, in the *cane*brakes.

Ruth I don't think so. Most of them are gone.
But we can think about them.

Pause.

Nick My father saw a bear once.

Ruth He did. Where?

Nick In the Black Forest.

Ruth In the War?

Nick Yes.

Ruth Tell me.

Nick Look. Look. Oh, my God.

Ruth What?

Pause.

Nick (*pointing*) The beaver.

Ruth Where?

Pause.

Where?

Nick I'm pointing at it.

Ruth I can't see it.

Nick There. Look. There.

Pause.

See?

Ruth Yes.

Nick Do you see?

Ruth Yes.

Nick No. You don't see where I'm pointing.

Ruth Yes. I do.

Nick You do?

Ruth Yes.

Pause.

Nick What?

Ruth It's a log.

Nick What is?

Ruth The beaver.

Pause.

Nick The beaver is?

Ruth Yes.

Nick No. You don't see where I'm pointing.

Ruth I don't think that we have beavers here.

Nick You don't see where I'm pointing.

Ruth Yes. I do.

Nick There? Near the raft?

Ruth Yes. It's a log.

Pause.

Nick It's a *log*?

Ruth I don't think we have beavers here.

Pause.

Nick But I swear I saw it swimming.

Ruth Sometimes something floats along it looks just like it's swimming.

Pause.

There's forces in the water.

Pause.

I know.
I used to fish for things when I was little.

Nick You did?

Ruth Yes. I did.

Nick For what?

Ruth These fish.
These lovely fish.

Nick What were they?

Ruth I don't know. I think that they were perch. They
tasted delicate. I used to clean them. I would get the smell
upon my hands. When I was little.
It smelled like I put my hands inside myself.
I used to like to clean the fish.
One time I sat down on the dock I lost this bracelet that my
Grandmother gave me.
It floated down.

Nick In summer?

Ruth Yes. In fall. I had the bracelet. I was on the dock.
(*Pause.*) I should not have been there.

Pause.

It fell.
It floated down. I dropped it.

Pause.

I can still see it.
Floating down.
It went so slowly.

Pause.

It was a necklace and I wore it as a bracelet.
Wrapped around.
My Grandmother's.

Pause.

Nick Nothing lasts forever.

Ruth We could do that.

Nick What, Ruth?

Ruth Wear things.

Nick What?

Ruth We could wear anything. Rings, bracelets.
Long, slim necklaces.
Gold necklaces.
We'd wear them on our wrists.

Pause.

Wrapped around.
To show that we are lovers.

Pause.

There are so many things that we could do.
I'm glad we came here.

Pause.

Do you know why I love it here?

Pause.

Nick Why?

Ruth Because it's clean.

Nick We used to come here all the time.

Ruth The winter, too?

Nick We'd drive up. In the winter. Summers.

Ruth You could come up any time you put up insulation.

Nick Yes.

Ruth And build the fires.

Nick We came up here.

Pause.

Ruth Did you?

Nick Many times.

Ruth Or maybe just the fireplace, you chinked it up.

Nick We used to see these men. At stoplights.
Way before the Superhighways.

Ruth (*to self*) That was a long time ago.

Nick They'd walk between the cars at stoplights . . . selling flowers to the men.

Ruth Huh!

Nick Sometimes they had boards with little animals.

Ruth No.

Nick Yes.

Ruth And they would sell them?

Nick Yes.

Ruth What happened to those men?

Nick I don't know. (*Pause.*)
Or paper boys, they used to walk between the rows.
They'd cry, 'All Late'.

Ruth 'All Late'.

Nick Yes.

Pause.

Ruth What did they mean?

Nick The papers were all late.

Ruth The papers were late.

Nick Yes.

Ruth The papers were late.

Nick Yes.

Pause.

Ruth They had a late edition.

Nick Yes. Or sometimes they would have balloons.

Ruth The paper boys?

Nick No.

Ruth No, I didn't think so.

Nick They would sell balloons.
Then you would go home.

Ruth I would love it up here in the winter.
(*To self.*) Buying toys or flowers for their family.

Nick Mmm.

Ruth We could sit and watch the snow and make a fire.
We could get a clock. We'd cuddle up inside our quilts and
watch the fire.

Nick We came up here in winter one time.
Many times.

Ruth You did?

Nick A few times.

Ruth Tell me.

Nick It was cold.

Ruth I know. I bet it was.

Nick We used to sit around, we'd make a fire.
Sometimes he'd tell us stories of the Indians, or from the
War.

Pause.

Ruth . . . sitting in the cold and he told stories from the
War.
I bet that you felt safe.

Nick We did.

Pause.

And content.

Ruth Because all things had stopped.

Nick What?

Ruth They had all stopped.
You were up here where you wished to be. (*Pause.*) Mmm.

Nick He used to sit out here all afternoon and work.

Pause.

In the summertime.
He'd weight the papers down with rocks.
He'd sit and work all afternoon.

Ruth You're like that, Nicky.

Nick I am?

Ruth I can watch you.

Nick . . . in his shirtsleeves.

Ruth . . . yes.
Because you are serene.

Pause.

I know what you are.

Pause.

I know.

Pause.

Nick I have to tell you something.

Pause.

Ruth Yes.

Nick I thought that was what life was.

Pause.

Ruth What was?

Pause.

Nick To be still.

Pause.

Ruth Not to want a thing. I know.

Nick To hear what did go on.
And be content.

Ruth Yes. It is like a brook. Yes.

Nick Do you know?

Ruth I do.

Nick And be content.

Ruth (*pause*) Tell me one.

Nick One what?

Ruth A story.

Nick No. I don't think that I ever tried to tell one.

Ruth No?

Nick Not one my father told.

Ruth Or *any* one.

Pause.

Try.
Or one he told you. Or about the Indians.

Nick *I* don't know . . .

Ruth Please. Please. You can. (*Pause.*) Please.
I know that you know them.
When you'd listen to them all those times.

Pause.

Please.

Nick Alright.

Ruth Oh, thank you. Good. This is the best. This is the best
thing two people can do.
To live through things together. If they share what they have
done before.

Nick *prepares to tell story*.

Nick Have you ever fallen from great distances?

Ruth What?

Nick Have you ever fallen from great distances?

Ruth This is the story?

Nick Yes.

Pause.

Ruth Good. Go on.

Pause.

Go *on*, Nick.

Pause.

Nick I'm not sure I remember.

Ruth Oh, don't tell me that. You do.

Nick I want to tell it right.

Ruth Well, tell it right, then. You can do it.

Nick Would you think a man's life could be saved by
someone's garter belt?

Ruth A man's or woman's garter belt?

Pause.

Nick Men do not wear garter belts.

Ruth They didn't then, though?

Nick No.

Ruth To hold their socks up?

Nick At their calves?

Ruth Yes.

Nick Those are just called 'garters'.

Pause.

Ruth I'm sorry. Go on, Nicky. Yes. I would believe it.
Have I ever fallen from great distances and lived.
(*Sotto, to self.*) This is the story.

Pause.

Nick In the War.
In The Black Forest.
Long ago.
My Dad went looking for a man he lost out on Patrol.
In winter.

Ruth Yes.

Nick His name was Herman Waltz.

Ruth (*to self*) Waltz.

Nick When the War was over, they would be involved together.

Ruth Uh-huh.

Nick He was nuts.

Ruth Waltz.

Nick Yes.

Ruth He was insane?

Nick Yes. He thought his head was a radio.
He had had dental work and said that Hitler told him things about his wife. Things he should do to her.
He later killed himself.

Ruth When?

Nick In the fifties.

Pause.

Ruth And he's in this same story?

Nick Yes.
He came up here. He said he had been kidnapped by the Martians.

Ruth No!

Nick Yes.

Ruth No.

Nick He said he'd driven up . . .

Ruth . . . Wait. Wait – he said the Martians kidnapped him up *here* . . . ?

Nick Yes.

Ruth No.

Nick He was on some road up here – he had come to see my Dad, he saw the lights.

He told us he had fallen from great distances.
Inside their craft.

Ruth (*softly, to self*) No.

Nick When they'd finished with him.

Ruth No.

Nick Yes.

Pause.

Ruth And you saw this man?

Nick I knew him. Yes.

Ruth (*to self*) He had been kidnapped by the Martians.

Nick He said that he had.

Ruth Did you believe him?

Nick Yes.

Long pause.

Ruth (*softly*) I know.

Nick He'd come up here . . . (*Pause.*) . . . he would be up here . . .

Ruth Yes. In the War, too.

Nick We do not know what goes on.

Ruth I know we do not.

Nick *Feelings, madness* . . .

Ruth (*softly*) Everything.

Nick The *Indians*.

Ruth That bear came back here.

Nick That bear here?

Ruth Yes.

Nick (*pause*) I'm sure it did.

Ruth They built the house upon its cave and it came back.

Nick I'm sure it did. These things go on.

Ruth I know they do.

Nick They all go on.

Pause.

All we have are insights.

Pause.

Who *knows* what's real?

Ruth Yes.

Nick They exist all independent of our efforts to explain them. Everything does. (*Pause.*) We cannot know it.

Pause.

My father. *Waltz.*

Pause.

They had *seen* things.

Pause.

Who knows. If they were real or not.

Ruth Yes.

Nick Whether they were real or not.

Pause.

He had had his insights.

Pause.

The things he saw. (*Pause.*) Whether he had imagined them or not. He had had insights.

Pause.

Do you know?

Ruth Yes.

Pause.

Nick You do?

Ruth Yes.

Pause.

Nick You know what I'm talking about?

Ruth Yes. I believe these things.

Pause.

Nick You see what I mean by his insights?

Ruth Yes.

Nick The *things* he'd seen.

Ruth I know.

Nick That Waltz had seen.

Ruth But we don't have to be afraid.
Because we have each other.

Pause.

Nick I'm not afraid.

Ruth Of course you're not. But I meant if you *were*.
As in a story. (*Pause.*)
Because we have each other.

Pause.

Will you take me in the house?
I want to lie down next to you.

Pause.

I want to hold you with my legs.
I want to stick my fingers in you.
I'm so glad we are here.
When I am with you, Nick, I feel so strong.
I feel like I know everything.

Pause.

I wish we could stay up here forever.

Nick You wouldn't like it.

Ruth No?

Nick No.

Ruth Yes, I would.

Nick You'd be bored.

Ruth No, I wouldn't. No.

Pause.

Why would I be bored?
I love it here.

Nick Things change.

Ruth In winter?

Nick Yes. In winter. *Many* times.

Ruth I know they do. That's why I like the country.
In the city we can never know each other really.

Pause.

It's clean out here.
And, plus, it's quiet.
Anything is possible. (*Pause.*)
You can see the way things are.

Nick Like what?

Ruth Like stars. (*Pause.*)
Like the way you look. (*Pause.*)
Many things. (*Pause.*)
Many things.
Can we go in now?

Nick Yes. (*He gets up.*)

Ruth And later, Nick . . . ?

Nick What?

Ruth I will give you something.

Nick What?

Ruth That I brought.

Nick You brought something for me?

Ruth Yes. A present.

Nick (*pause*) Thank you.

Ruth Well.

Pause.

Nick What is it?

Ruth A surprise.

Pause.

Something for you. (*They start to walk in.*)
Wait! Oh, wait!
How did they find that man?

Nick Who?

Ruth Herman.

Nick Herman Waltz.

Ruth How did they find him?

Pause.

Nick My Dad fell in a hole with him.

Ruth No!

Nick Yes.

Pause.

Ruth Will you tell me?

Pause.

Because I have to know it.

Nick Yes. I will.

Ruth No. Do you promise?

Nick Yes.

Ruth Good. (*Pause.*) Oh! I'm so happy, Nick.
I never had a place like this.
With porches. (*They continue going in.*)

Nick What did you bring me?

Ruth You will have to wait till later. (*She turns back.*)
'They had fallen in a hole.'

Nick They did.

Ruth Yes. (**Ruth** *turns. They go in.*)
You must tell me.

Scene 2

Night

Ruth *is sitting on a chair on the porch, looking out.* **Nick** *comes out.*

Nick (*enters*) My watch stopped.

Ruth Can't you sleep?

Nick What are you doing out here?

Ruth Sitting.

Nick Do you know what time it is?

Ruth No.

Pause.

Nick My watch stopped.

Ruth Can't you sleep?

Nick No. I woke up.

Pause.

Ruth Are you restless?

Nick I don't know what *time* it is . . .

Ruth Come here. Come here.

Pause. **Nick** *goes to her reluctantly.*

Ruth Did you have a bad dream?

Nick No. I was not dreaming. No.

Ruth Well, you're alright now.

Pause.

Nick I know.

Ruth You're alright. (*She begins to rock him. She holds him.*)
You are fine. (*Pause.*) Everything is just the way it should be.

Nick I can't sleep.

Ruth Why? Why, Babe?

Nick *I* don't know.

Ruth You want me to come back and hold you?

Nick No.

Ruth Alright.

Nick It's cold. It's going to rain.

Ruth I like it. I like Northern weather.

Nick Why?

Ruth It's clean.

Pause.

Nick I can't sleep.

Ruth Do you want to take a walk?

Nick Now?

Ruth Yes.

Pause.

Nick It's dark.

Ruth It's night.

Nick It's going to rain.
I don't want to go out there in the rain.

Ruth We'll wear the rain things.

Nick No. It's wet out there.

Ruth Come on.

Nick No.

Ruth We'll go put the rain stuff on and go out to the Point.

Nick No.

Ruth Where the old rowboat is.

Nick It isn't on the Point.

Ruth It's not? The rowboat?

Nick No.

Ruth I saw it out there.

Pause.

Nick The Point is over there. (*He points.*)

Ruth That's where the rowboat is.

Nick It is?

Ruth Yes.

Nick Then it's not our rowboat.

Ruth No?

Nick We kept our rowboat in the Cove.

Ruth It's not your rowboat?

Nick No.

Ruth Oh.

Pause.

Nick Is it blue?

Ruth It's a kind of blue.

Nick What is it?

Ruth Green.
It could of faded.

Nick What's it called?

Ruth I don't know.

Nick Did you see a name on it?

Ruth No. I don't think so.

Nick On the transom?

Ruth Near the back? The transom's near the back?

Pause.

The transom is the stern. Right, Nicky?

Nick Yes.

Ruth It's gone. It doesn't have one.
It got rotted off. I told you.

Pause.

What was yours called?

Nick I don't remember.

Ruth Let's go take a walk. We'll put the stuff on. Boots and stuff.

Nick There's lightning.

Ruth No, there isn't.

Nick Well, there will be.

Ruth I don't think it's coming here.

Nick You don't.

Ruth No. And it cannot kill you.

Nick It can't.

Ruth No.

Nick You think that it can't kill you?

Ruth No. It isn't going to hit you.
Come on, Nicky.

Nick I do not want to get wet.

Ruth You won't.

Nick I'm wet now, Ruth; it's blowing.

Pause.

Ruth Nick. It's lovely.
It is poetry.
The damp.

You know what this is? Bracing.
Coming on. We'll put stuff on and you'll like it.
It will be nice by the Point.

Nick It's night.

Ruth That's alright.
Are you hungry?

Nick No.

Ruth Well, I could put food on, and we'll go out and we'll
come back here and eat.
We'll have an appetite.

Pause.

We'll feel good.

Pause.

But we don't have to.

Nick If you want to, take a walk. It's alright.

Ruth Come *on*, Nick, I don't want to take one by *myself*, for
chrissake. (*Pause.*)
I want to be with *you* out there.
It will be wet, but we will not be *getting* wet. Our faces, just.
The two of us.
I always thought, I always wanted it to be like this.

Pause.

With my lover. In the country.
In the middle of the night. This is so beautiful.
Here we're awake. All by ourselves.
Oh, Nicky. All alone.

Pause.

Nick I'm glad that you're happy.

Pause.

Ruth Drip, drip, drip. The snow makes sound, too. Do you
think?

Nick I don't know.

Ruth We could sit out here in winter. We could watch the
snow come down. Huh?
What about that?
Bundled up in coats and blankets with our scarf around our
neck and stocking hats. Huh?

Pause.

Wouldn't that be funny?

Nick Yes, that would.

Ruth Just sitting out here on the winter.
Bundled up. Not moving.
Like some married couple in a picture.
Rocking back and forth.

Pause.

Come here. Come here.
Oh, you're sleepy.
Come here and I'll tell a story. (*He moves close to her.*)
I will tell a story and then we can go to sleep.
I'm going to tell a bedtime story.

Nick Alright.

Ruth That my Grandmother told me.
You would of loved her. I think.
She was old.

Nick How old was she?

Ruth Well, she was old. When she died, she was eighty-six.
She saw a lot of things.
She always told us bedtime stories.
And then we would go to sleep.
Come here.

Nick Is it wet?

Ruth No. No. I'm going to keep you dry.

Nick I'll get wet.

Ruth No, you won't.

Nick It's going to blow all over me.

Ruth I'll shield you, come here. (*Pause.*)
It's going to blow the other way.

Nick How do you know?

Ruth I know.

Nick How?

Ruth Because I just know. (*Pause. He goes to her.*)

Ruth Now, this feels better. We could never do this in the city. Are you comfortable?

Nick Yes.

Ruth Good.

Pause.

There was the moon and wolves and these old women and small children.

Nick (*softly*) It's dry here.

Ruth I told you.
And there always was a moon . . .
A crescent moon . . . a new moon . . .
What's a new moon?

Nick I don't know.

Ruth Does it mean big or small?

Nick I don't know.

Pause.

Ruth And I was always in them. And my brother.
She would tell us – now relax.
One day at dinnertime, these children had gone to their Granma's house. They loved her very much. While she was cooking, they asked could they go and play – the house was near the woods – and she said yes, they could, but that they had these *wolves* in them, and bears lived in them, too.

Nick Some brown bears.

Ruth Yes.

Nick Some European Brown Bears.

Ruth Now, be quiet. So we must be careful in the woods.
We had to take care of each other, and be very careful not to
go too far.
The moon came up. The breezes blew.
The sun was going down.
The little children went into the woods.
It became cold.
They found that they had lost their way.
They could not see the moon.
Birds called to one another.

Pause.

'The Sun is Down.'
The rain began to fall . . .
Oh, Nicky, are you sleeping?

Nick No.

Ruth You want to take a walk?

Nick No.

Pause.

I have to ask you something.

Ruth What?

Nick Do you like it up here?

Ruth Yes.

Pause.

Nick What happened when you got there?

Ruth When we got inside?

Nick Yes.

Ruth In the woods . . .
We became lost.
We lost our way. (*To self.*) The sun is down, the rain began to
fall. (*Aloud.*) I think that always at the end our parents found
us in the morning.

Pause.

Although I don't remember.

Nick Is she dead now?

Ruth Granma?
Yes. She died.

Pause.

Nick Do you miss her?

Ruth Very much. I miss her all the time.
I think about her. (*Pause.*)
I lost her bracelet. That her husband gave her.
Well, I told you.

Pause.

I dropped it in the Lake.
I can still see it.
Falling.
Falling.
Are you cold?

Nick A little.

Pause.

My father fell into this old abandoned mine with Herman
Waltz.

Ruth Uh-huh.

Nick Waltz told him that they'd never leave that hole alive.

Ruth And how deep was it?

Nick Deep. Deep. Very deep.

Ruth Did they have stuff to eat?

Nick No. (*Pause.*) And they were cold.

Ruth I *bet* they were.

Nick And battered.

Pause.

Ruth How long did they stay down there?

Nick And the rain fell.

Pause.

Ruth And they were down there how long?

Pause.

Nick They got out that afternoon.

Ruth Oh.

Pause.

Nick The rescue party found them.

Ruth Mmm.

Nick It rained the whole time.

Ruth Many times the best and worst things happen over just a little while.

Nick My Dad said all he talked about was his new wife.

Ruth Waltz.

Nick In Chicago. How he'd never see his wife again.

Ruth Sometimes when you stay up you get these visions.

Nick Do you want a drink?

Ruth Sure.

Nick *goes inside.*

Nick (*from inside*) When he got back to Chicago, he would beat her up.

Ruth What?

Pause. **Nick** *comes out with bottle.*

Nick He used to beat her up.

Ruth He used to beat his *wife* up?

Nick Yes.

Pause.

Ruth Why?

Nick I don't know.

Ruth Oh.

Pause.

Nick He was crazy.

Ruth (*to self*) Yes.

Nick My Dad said he was an unhappy man.

Ruth This is the man that saw the Martians.

Nick Yes.

Ruth He said he saw them here.

Nick Near here.

Ruth (*to self*) Actually right near here. (*Pause. She drinks.*) I like this stuff.

Nick Uh-huh.

Ruth My Granma never slept.
She had this couch out by the windows and she had a quilt.

Nick *takes bottle.*

Ruth She'd keep the window open. We were on the first floor. Sometimes I would see her in the morning, all wrapped up in her quilt and looking out the window.
She would tell these stories.
They had Cossacks.
They had bears there.
People were escaping and she hid them underneath her petticoats. They took them all to safety through the Forest.

Pause.

Nick (*to self*) That *could* of been our rowboat . . .

Ruth She loved her husband very much.
He was killed.

Nick What was he?

Ruth A blacksmith. He was older than her.

Nick What did he die of?

Ruth He was killed. I used to ask my mother how come she was sitting in the window.
She just sat there. Granma.
She would tell me, in the winter, they would make love. Him and her. For hours.

Nick Your grandmother told you?

Ruth Yes.

Nick How old were you?

Ruth I don't know.
They would lay in bed.
I saw the Photographs of what she looked like. And of him.
When she was little, too.
She looked like me.
She said he was like Iron. He could lift her in one hand.
They'd lie in bed all day and never speak . . . they'd take long walks.

Pause.

Oh, she told me many times. The way his hair smelled.
In the rain.
The singed forearms. The smell . . .

Pause.

Granma married this man in Chicago.

Pause.

He was a nice man. Jacky Weiss.

Pause.

But she missed her husband so. She used to watch the window in the snow. It was cold. You could hear her whispering. I don't know. Maybe she was praying.

Pause.

She loved him. They were married.
Nothing, even he was crippled – or she was – could separate them.

She was his. Forever.
They had made a vow.

Nick (*to self*) Some pagan vow.

Pause.

Ruth He gave that necklace to her.
Can you think, Nick?
All the secrets, all the things they shared?
At night. In bed.

Pause.

She was like the Earth.
She knew so many things.
I think about her all the time.
I wish I had not lost her bracelet.

Pause.

She used to wear it.

Pause.

Nick Who killed him?

Ruth I don't know.
Some farmer.

She takes wine. Drinks.

(*She declaims.*) Wine, wine, wine.
The Earth. The Sky. The Rain.

Nick The Water.

Ruth Yes.

Pause.

Nick Women are immortal.

Ruth No. They have no sense of values.
No, I know.

Pause. She goes over to an oar.

An oar. What is this? It goes in the oarlock. What is it called?

Nick An oarlock pin.

Pause.

Ruth (*to self*) Oarlock pin.
This thing could be the color of the boat. This is from your boat?

Nick Yes.

Ruth Then I think it's the same one. I think it is.

Nick It's going to come down.

Ruth To really come down.

Nick Yes.

Ruth The rain.
The water brings the fishes out.

Pause.

After the rain they huddle near the surface.

Pause.

And then you can catch them.
Fish come up for insects. When the storm is over.

Nick For the larvae.

Ruth Larvae?

Nick Yes.

Ruth The little insects?

Nick Yes.

Ruth The fish come up to eat them?

Nick Yes.

Ruth I know they do.

Pause.

Drip drip. Rain comes down, drip. It makes rings. It makes these circles.
Ripples. Plop. A fish comes up. Fishes come up. They make the same ripples from underneath.

Pause.

Nick Larvae are really eggs.

Ruth I know that.

Pause.

I used to say that we are only fish beneath the sea. I read this book when I was small – it said that we live in an ocean made of air and we are only fish beneath the sea.

Nick You said that?

Ruth Yes. You know, except we couldn't *swim* or anything. (*Pause.*) You want to come with me on my walk?

Big lightning flash.

Look at *that!*

Nick Lightning.

Ruth Jesus, Nicky, huh?

Nick (*to self*) A storm.

Ruth I bet that you watched them a lot. Storms.
If I was out here, I would sit all day.
I would.
We always used to know, it rained, the thing we had to do was go and put the boats onto their side. To turn them upside-down.
You know?
You ever sit inside a boat that way?
Some rowboat or canoe?

Nick Yes.

Pause.

Ruth It's nice.

Nick Yes.

Ruth All *warm* . . .
Look at that!
The wind howls and howls, but you're warm.

Nick I'd sit here.

Ruth Yes.

Nick And think about things like that.

Ruth Would you? (*Pause.*) What things?

Nick You know.

Pause.

Ruth Tell me.

Nick Homes and things.

Ruth When the storms blew.

Nick Yes.

Ruth What about them?

Nick Living in them. Being warm.

Pause.

Ruth Being in them with somebody.

Nick Yes.

Ruth Please tell me.

Nick I don't know.

Pause.

Ruth Tell me.

Nick Just these thoughts I had.

Ruth When you would settle down.

Nick Yes.

Ruth Here?

Nick I don't know.

Ruth Who with?

Pause.

Nick I don't know.

Ruth And what would you think?

Nick How it would be.

Ruth How would it be?

Nick I don't know.

Ruth Yes. You do. Tell me.

Nick I don't know.

Ruth Please tell me. (*Pause.*) Please tell me. (*Pause.*) *Please.*

Pause.

Nick We would meet.

Ruth Uh-huh.

Nick And . . . you know, we would meet and we would just be happy.

Ruth You would.

Nick Yes.

Pause.

Ruth What, with Houses?

Nick Yes.

Ruth Here?

Nick No.

Pause.

Ruth *Some*where.

Nick Yes. And maybe it was raining.

Ruth It was raining?

Nick In my dream.

Ruth When you would be with someone.

Pause.

Nick Do you think that is childish?

Ruth What?

Nick *Day*dreaming.

Ruth No.

Nick You don't?

Ruth Not if you thought it. (*Pause.*) But sometimes things are different than the way you thought they'd be when you set out on them.
This doesn't mean that, *you* know, that they aren't . . . that they aren't . . . Wait. Do you know what I mean?

Nick No.

Ruth That they aren't *good*.
Just because they're different.

Pause.

Nick What's your surprise?

Ruth Things can be unexpected and be beautiful if we will let them. (*Pause.*) And not be frightened by them. Nick.

Nick What did you bring me?

Ruth I will tell you later.
Do you understand me?

Nick No.

Ruth You do, though.

Pause.

You don't have to be nervous when a thing is new.

Nick I am not nervous.

Ruth No, but that is all I mean. (*Pause.*) Sometimes things are different.

Pause.

Nick This drink is good.

Ruth I know. Drink it. It's good.
Do you know what I mean?
We all have fantasies.
And dreams.
I have them.

Many things I want.

Pause.

Or would dream about.
I know they can be frightening.
To do them.

Pause.

I know.

Nick You know that, eh?

Pause.

Ruth What?

Pause.

Lightning flash.

The lightning doesn't look like anything.
Do you know what I mean?

Nick No.

Pause.

Ruth It doesn't 'look' like anything.

Pause.

Do you know what I mean?

Nick No. (*He chuckles.*)

Ruth What's funny?

Nick Nothing.

Ruth All I meant, like clouds, or something.
They look like something.
You know what I meant.

Nick I'm sorry.

Pause.

Ruth I wasn't trying to be funny.

Nick I know.

Ruth Then you shouldn't *laugh* at me.
Do you think that I'm funny? Huh?
I know I'm funny *sometimes* . . .

Pause.

There's nothing wrong in being serious.

Nick I'm sorry.

Pause.

Ruth It's alright.

Pause.

I understand. (*She starts to go.*)

Nick You going?

Ruth Yes.

Nick Hold on. I'm sorry.

Ruth I'm just going for my walk.

Nick Where are you going?

Ruth By the Lake.

Nick Come here a minute.

Ruth What?

Nick Come here.

Ruth I'll be back in a while.
I'll be right back. (*Pause.*) I'm getting sticky in this suit if I'm
not in the rain.

Nick Come here.
I want to tell you something. Sit down.

Pause.

Ruth You want me to sit down now?

Nick Yes.

Ruth Alright. (*She sits down.*)

Nick I'm sorry that I laughed at you.

Ruth No. That's alright. I understand. (*She gets up to go.*)

Nick Hold on.

Ruth I'll be back. I just want to be out there with the lightning.

Nick Come here. (*He begins to pull her down to the floor.*)

Ruth What? It's wet. (**Nick** *begins making sexual overtones.*)

Nick Mmm.

Ruth It's wet. This stuff is sticky.

Nick You smell good.

Ruth I was out in the sun today. Come on, the floor is wet, Nick.

Nick Lift up.

Ruth I'll be back. Just let me go, and I'll come back.

Nick Come on.

Ruth Alright. We'll go inside. (*She starts to get up.*)

Nick Lift up a minute.

Ruth Wait. Hold on. We'll go inside.

Nick This is all knotted.

Ruth Hold on, Nick.

He tears her pants off.

You tore 'em, will you hold *on*, for chrissake? This thing is rough.

He kicks over the bottle.

You're knocking the *bottle*.
Alright. Alright.
Wait.
Just hold on a second.

He pushes the rainshell up over her face.

Just a second. Oh. Okay. Hold on a second, though.

He prepares to mount her.

No, *wait!*
Wait.
I can't *see!*
No. Wait. (*She fights the shell down and maneuvers a little way away from him.*)

Pause.

I'll go inside. I'll get some stuff.

Pause.

Do you want me to go get some stuff? (*Pause.*)

Nick (*of rainwear*) This shit is all mildewed.

Ruth Do you want me to go in and get some stuff?

Nick (*to self*) How can you wear this?

Ruth I'll go right in and get it.

Pause.

I'll get the stuff.

Nick No.

Ruth I will.

Nick No.

Ruth Are you sure?

Pause.

Nick Where's the bottle?

Ruth I don't know. (*She looks for bottle.*)

Nick Do you know, there's nothing to do here.

Ruth Well, that isn't my fault. Nicky.

Nick I didn't say it was your fault.

Ruth Yes. You did. There's lots to do here.
We could walk around. I walked around.
There's lots to do. You said that you liked thunderstorms.
There's lots of things to do. Don't tell me that.

Pause.

You're mad because I wasn't wet.

Nick No. I'm not.

Ruth You are. You pushed me, though.

Nick I'm sorry.

Ruth (*to self*) Yeah.

Nick I'm sorry.

Pause.

Ruth You can't, just because you know, just because you *want* something . . . There is a way things are.

Nick Mmm.

Ruth You know?

Nick No. What in the world are you talking about?

Ruth That you're mad 'cause I wasn't wet.

Nick That isn't true.

Ruth You think that means I do not want you.

Nick No.

Ruth You do.

Nick I know that it doesn't mean that.

Ruth No, you don't.

Nick I do.

Ruth Yeah?

Nick I know that you want me.

Ruth I *do* want you.

Nick I know that.

Ruth But you just can't push me *around*.

Nick I know.

Ruth You don't. You're all inside this thing you're in. A shell, or something. You can't see. This is no good. No. If you come up here with me, that means you are . . .

Pause.

Nick What?

Ruth What? Nothing.

Nick What did you say?

Pause.

Ruth I didn't.

Nick Yes, you did. What did you say? (*Pause.*) You tell me what you said.

Ruth I said – I said – that when you come up here that means you are committed.

Nick Oh.

Ruth Yes. If you are a man. Because I am your guest.

Nick (*to self*) If I'm a man.

Ruth And you know how I want you, so don't tell me you're mad that I'm not wet. Don't tell me that. But you, you do not treat me with respect.

Nick Will you shut up one second, please?

Pause.

You talk too much, Ruth.

Ruth I don't.

Nick Why don't you take your walk?

Ruth Why don't *you?*

Pause.

I'll shut up, you want me to shut up?
I'll shut up. (*Pause. Of oar.*) Why is this all burnt?

Nick I used to use it in the winters when I stirred the fire up.

Ruth When you would *come* up here.

Pause.

Nick Yes.

Ruth When you would come up here with other people.

Pause.

Nick Yes.

Ruth Oh.

Pause.

You frightened me.

Nick I'm sorry.

Ruth I came here, and then you acted funny.
I thought that we were both in this together.

Nick *drinks.*

Ruth May I have some? (*He gives her wine. Pause.*)

Nick I'm sorry.

Ruth Yeah. Oh, well. That's alright. These things have to come out.

Pause.

Nick I'm sorry, Ruth.

Ruth Okay. (*They sit down.*)

Nick What have you got for me?

Ruth I have a lot of things for you. I have so many things. You don't know. I'm not who you think I am, Nick.

Pause.

Nick What is the present?

Pause.

I meant the present.

Ruth I know what you mean. I am not stupid. Do you want it?

Nick Yes.

Ruth Are you sure?

Nick Yes.

Ruth Alright.

Nick What is it?

Ruth I am going to give it to you. (*She gets up.*)

Nick Wait.

Ruth What?

Nick I don't know.

Ruth What? (*Pause.*) You don't know what?

Nick I don't know if I want it.

Ruth Oh.

Pause.

Oh.
You are so dumb sometimes. My God.
You are so dumb.

Nick All of this *rain* . . .

Ruth Well, it's *raining*. That's got nothing to do, rain, with anything.

Nick We sat out here.

Ruth (*to self*) We're sitting out here *now* . . .

Nick And read.

Ruth You read books.

Nick Or told stories. We came up here with our friends.

Pause.

Ruth Are you lonely?

Nick I would look up at the stars.

Ruth Uh-huh. (*Pause.*) Are you lonely?

Nick I don't know.

Pause.

Ruth Do you want me to go home?

Nick I don't know.

Pause.

Ruth Why can't you sleep?

Nick I don't know.

Ruth Yes. You do. What is it?

Nick Nothing.

Ruth Yes, it is. (*Pause.*) Tell me.

Nick No, it's not anything. I'm sorry . . .
Come here . . .

Ruth Are you mad at me?

Nick No.

Ruth Do you want to go in?

Nick No.

Pause.

Ruth What *do* you want?

Pause.

Come on, we'll go inside.

Nick Why?

Ruth I don't know. We'll make a sandwich.

Nick Why?

Ruth Because if you were hungry.

Nick Well, I'm not.

Ruth Okay. Okay. We have to talk.
I have to talk to you. (*Pause.*)
Gimme some.

Nick You're drunk.

Ruth I am not. Gimme some. Gimme some. (*He gives her some wine.*)
Alright. Siddown. Look: Are you cold?

Nick Yes.

Ruth Alright, then. Look. You stay here.
I am going to get you something.
Stay here. (*She goes inside, and comes out and hands him a package.*)
This is for you.

Pause.

Nick What is it?

Ruth Just open it. (*Pause.*)
Open it, and then we'll talk.

He opens it. He takes out a bracelet. He examines it.

Nick It's very nice. (*Pause. He continues to examine the bracelet.*)
Is it gold?

Pause.

Ruth Read it.

Nick 'Nicholas. (*Pause.*) I will always love you, Ruth.'

A long pause.

Ruth Put it on.

Nick (*very softly*) No.

Ruth Then go fuck yourself. Look: You don't understand.
You don't know me. You don't.
You think that I'm stupid. You do.
You think that. *Don't* you?

Nick No.

Ruth Yeah, you do. You don't know, you don't know a
thing. Look. Look. Look, Nick.
I love you. I love you so much. I just want to be with you.
That's the only thing I want to do. I do not want to hurt you.

Pause.

Do you want to make love to me?
Nick?
Do you want to make love?

Pause.

Nick No.

Pause.

Ruth You don't want to make love to me?

Nick No.

Ruth You know that I want you, Nick. You know that.

Pause.

Why do you think I came up with you?

Nick Why?

Ruth Do you *care?*

Nick Why did you come up?

Ruth You don't know why I did? Are you *dumb?* What do you mean?

Pause.

Caw, caw, caw, the gulls fly.
They eat fish?

Nick I don't know.

Ruth They either eat the fish or insects. (*Pause.*)
We eat fish. The fish eat seaweed.
It all dies, the things turn into shells.

Pause.

Or deposits. They wash up. As coral.
Maybe they make sand, or special beaches.
They decay and wash away.

Pause.

Then they form the islands.

Pause.

Nothing lasts forever.

Pause.

Don't make me go home.

Pause.

I want to live with you. Go put it on.

Nick I know some things that you don't know.

Ruth You know what?

Nick Things.

Ruth Things.

Pause.

You don't know *any*thing.

Pause.

You don't even know what's *good* for you, you come up here with all those others, I don't know, and the only woman who loves you and you don't know *shit*. You think I'm stupid.

Pause.

You never had this. *You're* the one that's stupid.

Nick Do you know that you demean yourself?

Ruth I do.

Nick Yes.

Ruth Isn't that too bad.

Nick It is.

Ruth You don't have any feelings.

Nick I have feelings.

Ruth What are they?

Pause.

What are they?
You *think* that you have feelings.
Why do we come up here if you're so upset the whole time, that's what I would like to know.

Nick Why?

Pause.

Ruth You *asked* me, I am your guest up here.
You're bored or what, what am I s'posed to do, go off and
drown myself somewhere?
I am your guest.
We could be many things to one another.

Pause.

In our friendship.
You have no idea of the possibilities.

Pause.

Do you know that?

Nick Why don't you leave me alone?

Pause.

Ruth I will. (*Pause.*) I don't like to be in places where I don't
feel good.
When's the next bus?

Nick In the morning.

Ruth Well, I'm going to take it. So that's it.
So you can just relax. I've had enough of this. (*Pause.*)
Life goes on.
Drip *drip*.
Drip *drip*.
Do you feel better now?

Nick Yes.

Ruth Good. (*Pause.*) I care how you feel.
We have to learn from things. (*Pause.*) Do you think that?

Nick Yes. I do.

Ruth Yes, I do, too. (*Pause.*)
Many things go on.
We have to learn from them. Good. Good.
Your friend saw Martians here.

Nick My father's friend.

Ruth You think that there are Martians?

Nick On Earth?

Ruth Yes.

Nick There might be.

Ruth But what do you *think?*

Nick I don't know, Ruth.

Ruth Inside our ocean made of air?

Nick I don't know, for God's sake. (*He gets up.*)

Ruth What would you do if you, you know, if you came across them?
You think you'd be scared?

Pause.

If you saw a Martian?
Or a ghost.
Some vision?

Nick Of what?

Ruth I don't know.
You said that you thought they came among us.
They could do that.
They could infiltrate our people.

Nick I am getting wet.

Ruth Please. I have to ask you, they could monitor us.
They could send down members of their company to live here.
They would look like you and me.

Nick *gets up and starts to go in.*

Ruth Please. Wait. I'm telling you.
I'm telling you this story.
We would come into the kitchen, we would hang our hat up,
'Hi, Babe . . . did you have a good day?'
But there wouldn't be an answer.

Pause. **Nick** *gets up.*

Ruth Please, please, I have to tell you this.
Because there was no one *there*.

Pause.

They played upon us.
We had been alone the whole time.
We had wanted it for so long that they came and they knew
our desires.
There was no one there.

Pause. **Nick** *shakes his head.*

Ruth What?

Nick You have no idea what you're saying.

Ruth I don't.

Nick Not at all.

Pause.

Not at all.

Pause. They sit for a moment then she gets up to go in.

Where are you going?

Ruth In. I have to pack.

Scene 3

Morning

Ruth It's rotten when you don't feel good. I know.

Pause.

Do you want some more coffee?

Nick No.

Pause.

Ruth Would you like to take a walk?

Nick It's all wet.

Ruth We could put our boots on.

Nick I don't think so.

Pause.

Ruth (*of jacket*) Your Dad wore this in the War, huh?

Nick No. I don't feel good.

Ruth I know.

Nick He wore another one.

Ruth We could go down by the Point. Down there. (*Of oar.*) Do these things float?

Nick Unless they're waterlogged.

Ruth Is this one?

Nick No. It's burnt.

Ruth You're tired.

Nick Yes.

Ruth Well, later you can take a nap.

Nick I think I will.

Ruth If we go to take a walk, you might get tired out.

Nick No. Please, no.

Ruth I'm sorry.

Pause.

Nick I'm not glad that you're going.

Ruth We don't have to become morbid.

Nick We can see each other.

Ruth Back there?

Nick Yes.

Pause.

Ruth Nicky, Nicky, Nicky.

Nick No?

Pause.

We used to have all these different animals up here.

Ruth Uh-huh.

Nick Blue herons. Beavers.

Ruth I don't think that you had beavers here.

Nick Well, we did. The herons flew along.
They flew along at sunset. I would watch them.

Ruth Herons. They still have them?

Nick I don't know. They fly so slowly.
And their wings touch down and make two circles.

Ruth Mmm.

Nick Their feet drag.

Pause.

We caught this raccoon one time in a milk crate.

Pause.

Ruth You told me.

Nick Yes.

Pause.

I'll call you up.

Pause.

I'll call you when you get back.

Ruth Mm.

Nick No?

Ruth Come on.

Nick What?

Ruth You know.

Nick What?

Ruth Nothing changes just because you move it somewhere else.

Nick I'll call you.

Ruth Yeah. Don't.

Pause.

I'm sorry.

Nick Alright.

Ruth You know. It gets cold.

Nick Mm.

Ruth We put clothes on.

Nick Uh-huh.

Ruth Yes. I've got to tell you: We put on clothes, we can not make out what we look like.

Pause.

We make mistakes. We all get guarded.

Pause.

It's very lonely, and we all get desperate to be warm.
We have to find our lovers when it's warm.
We look at people and we see the things they are.
When they are on the Beach, or when they're happy.

Pause.

Some things that look like maybe they'd be good for us.

Pause.

It gets real cold up here until the fog burns off.

Nick Mmm.

Ruth You need insulation.

Nick Well, we're right up on the Lake.

Pause.

Ruth Yes.

Pause.

Nick We had talked about it at one time.

Ruth The thing about fish, they stay down there, it makes no difference to them.

Nick Waves don't make a difference.

Ruth What?

Nick The waves don't make a difference.

Pause.

They're on the surface, but they don't affect the water underneath.

Ruth They don't?

Nick No.

Ruth Currents, only, right?

Pause.

I don't know, I don't know.
Everything gets over.

Pause.

You know?
We all try to be very brave. What do you call it when you try not to show anything?

Nick I don't know.

Pause.

Ruth We all try to be warriors. Or pirates, something.
They all used to go to sea and rape the cabin boys. The Vikings.

Pause.

The worst part, maybe, is just learning little *things*.
The *things* about each other. Other people.

Pause.

Like if they play the piano.
Until you have taken care of them when they are sick.
The way their sweat tastes.

Pause.

Those are the worst things.

Nick We could call each other up.

Ruth Oh, you're so sorry sometimes.

Nick I am.

Ruth Yes.

Nick Do you want some more coffee?

Ruth No.

Nick You have a hangover?

Ruth No.

Nick Do we have an aspirin?

Ruth I don't know.

Nick You hungry?

Ruth No. Are you?

Nick I don't know.

Ruth I might have an aspirin in my bag.

Nick It's all packed.

Ruth I'll get it.

Nick No. What time is it?

Ruth Eight-thirty.

Pause.

Nick Do you want to go inside and lie down for a while?

Ruth No.

Nick Did you get any sleep?

Ruth I didn't want to sleep.

Nick You could go in and take a nap. I'll wake you.

Ruth I can nap on the way back.

Nick What will you do when you get back?

Ruth I don't know.

Nick Do you want to call me up to tell me you got in alright?

Ruth No.

Nick Did you take your wet stuff?

Ruth Yes.

Nick There's any stuff you want to leave, I'll bring it in.

Ruth Why would I want to leave it?

Pause.

Nick To dry.

Ruth It's alright.

Nick Call me up tonight to tell me you got in alright.

Ruth I have things that I have to do.

Nick Oh.

Pause.

I'll think about you.

Ruth Will you.

Nick Yes.

Ruth You'll think about me while you're here.

Nick Yes.

Pause.

Ruth I bet.

Nick I will.

Ruth The gulls fly. Caw, Caw, Caw. And winter comes and they go somewhere else.
Do they go somewhere else when winter comes?

Nick I don't know.

Ruth You were up here.

Nick Well. I don't remember.

Ruth All the times that you came up here?

Nick I didn't come up here that many times.

Ruth No, huh?

Nick No.

Ruth In winter.

Nick No.

Ruth With all your little memories.

Nick What memories?

Ruth About things.

Nick What things?

Ruth Everything. I don't know. (*Pause.*) I'm going swimming.

Nick It's too cold.

Ruth It's not. The water still stays warm.

Nick The air.

Ruth I'll dry off.

Nick It might rain again.

Ruth Uh-huh. What? Lightning's going to kill me?

Pause.

Nick Why are you going swimming?

Ruth To wake up.

Nick It's filthy. All the beach is mud.
The water is all muddy. (*Pause.*) Huh?

Ruth Just leave me to be by myself for a minute.

Nick You want me to come with you?

Ruth No.

Nick You sure?

Ruth I'm, yeah, I'm sure. Yeah. What time is it?

Nick Your suit will be cold.

Ruth Mm.

Nick Don't wear it, it will just get wet again.

Ruth You want me to go down there naked?

Nick Yes.

Ruth Fuck you.

Pause.

Nick Why do you say that?

Ruth I don't have to tell you.

Nick What, your body? (*Pause.*)
I want to see your body?
That's why I tell you to go down there?

Pause.

I can see your body anytime I want to.
Isn't that a little bit ridiculous?
Don't you think that that's a little silly?

Ruth (*pause*) If you say so.

Nick I can see your body anytime I want to. (*Pause.*) Can't
I?

Ruth You know that is all gone, Nicky.

Nick That's all gone?

Ruth That is all over now.

Nick It is?

Ruth You know it is. If I stay in too long, will you call down
for me?

Nick Stay here a second.

Ruth What? I'm freezing, what?

Nick Come here.

Ruth What?

Nick Just come here. I want to talk to you.

Ruth Come *on* now, Nicky.

Nick Come here.

Ruth Oh, just *stop* it, huh? Just *stop* it.

Nick What?

Ruth Grow up. (*He goes to her.*)

Nick Does that feel good?

Ruth Please.

Nick Doesn't that feel good?

Ruth For Christ's sake, *stop* it!

Nick Let's go upstairs.

Ruth Come on, Nick.

Nick Let's do it.

Ruth I'm – just grow up – I am going swimming. *Please*. (*She moves away from him.*)

Nick Come upstairs with me.

Ruth Will you come and call me in a half an hour?

Nick I want you to come upstairs with me. I want to fuck you.

Pause.

Ruth That's charming.

Nick Is it?

Ruth Yes. It is.

Nick I want to fuck you.

Ruth Well, you just go fuck your*self*. I'm going swimming.

Nick What did you say?

Ruth I said you can fuck your *own* self.

Nick (*pause*) You're so full of shit.

Ruth I'm what?

Nick Okay. Okay. Go.

Ruth What? I'm full of shit?

Nick Go. Go on. Go. I'll call you. (*Pause.*) Go in the water.

Ruth Wait. I'm full of shit about what? (*Pause.*)
You have bizarre ideas, you know? (*Pause.*)
With your fantasies. You're goddamn *right* go fuck yourself.
Go up here all the time – I don't know – some poor babe you
get to come here you can stick your fingers in them and you
tell them how Your Father Fought in World War Two.
And those dumb Martians. You're so fucking corny.
You don't belong *here* . . .
You don't even know the things are *good* for you.
You do not know what's going *on* . . . (*Pause.*)
Your father and that guy they sat – You're so afraid of
everything –
You make this manly stuff up . . .
Him and that guy with the Martians, they were going to die.
Inside that hole.
What did they *think* of?
When they talked about their broads.
When they were going to die?
You stupid shit.
. . . sucking each other off inside that hole . . .
Who did they *think* of?

Pause.

When they were dead?
You stupid shit.

Nick Shut up.

Ruth There *are* no men.

Nick Shut up.

Ruth You don't know *dick*. And I respected you, too. (*She
snorts.*) You lure the poor babes up here in the winter and you
roll around and tell them of the Indians. You fuck them and
you send them home.
I hope you're very happy. (*Pause.*) You don't deserve me.

Nick Me. I don't deserve you.

Ruth No. You don't.

Nick You're *nothing*, honey.

Ruth YES, I AM.

Nick You're nothing with your cheapjack shit.

He throws bracelet which has been on table down to floor.

This talk is cheap. This sentiment.
You're *nothing*. And do you know why?

Ruth No.

Pause.

Nick You have no self-respect.

Ruth I don't.

Nick No.

Pause.

Ruth And then I'm not worth anything. (*Pause.*) So that when you get – I don't know – when you become bored, I am supposed to pack up and go off.
To not upset you.
I am supposed to go and drown myself.
And if I don't, I've got no self-respect.

Pause.

Nick That's right.

Ruth *goes to oar, takes it and swings it viciously at him.*

Ruth I hope you die.

He parries the blow and hits her in the mouth. She falls off the porch.
Pause.

Ruth You don't like women.

Nick Are you alright?

Ruth You do not respect me.

Pause.

Nick Are you alright?

Ruth I don't think that you like women.

Nick Are you alright? (*Pause.*) I'm sorry.

Ruth You do not respect me at all.

Nick Did I hurt you?

Ruth I don't know . . .

Nick *goes to her.*

Ruth Please. Please don't touch me. I am going home.
This is wet. This is all wet.
I'm going home.

Nick Let me come and dry you off.

Ruth No. I'm alright. I'm alright here.

Pause.

Nick Did I hurt you?

Ruth No.

Nick Good.

Pause.

Ruth (*to self*) Oh, who can know what I should do here?

Pause.

Nick Ruth, what did I do to you?

Ruth (*to self*) Ruth.

Nick Did I hurt you?

Ruth (*to self*) This is all wet.

Nick I got nuts.

Ruth We look back, we look back at things. The things that
we knew. About each other.

Nick Come in.

Ruth All those things we knew.

Nick You're going to catch your death.

Ruth The Lake. Those things live down there.

Nick What things?

Ruth The Plankton.

Nick Aren't you wet?

Ruth The screaming.

Nick Come up.

Ruth Blood. Your tongue. (*Pause.*) When I had you in me
the first time. (*Pause.*) When you had me. (*Pause.*) Must I be
punished? (*She starts to cry.*)

Nick Things change. Oh, this is no good.

Ruth That's why I wanted to *come* here.
To get back to Nature.
We can't do that in the City. (*Pause.*)
But we could do that *here.*
You said you loved me.

Nick When?

Ruth That time.

Nick When?

Ruth You remember.

Nick No.

Ruth You do.

Nick I don't remember.

Ruth Yes, you do.
I wouldn't lie about that.

Pause.

Nick I don't remember.

Ruth Yes. You told me.

Pause.

Nick When? *When?*

Ruth And we watched the lightning.

Pause.

I guess you're always better off to be the other one.
She said that when the Polack knifed him, all the clocks
stopped. On her locket.
The grandfather clock. They would not tell the time.
(*Pause.*) Jacky Weiss said that was just a pile of shit.
He hit him with a pitchfork in the chest.
She loved him, though. She always loved him. (*Pause.*)
I think my shoulder hurts.

Nick You want me to put something on it?

Ruth No.

Nick A bandage. (*Pause.*) Mercurochrome?

Ruth Mercurochrome is only water.

Nick Iodine? Some iodine?

Ruth *starts to cry.*

Ruth (*to self*) This *mud* . . .

Nick I'm sorry, Ruth.

Ruth Yeah. We will hang on to each other.
You don't want to know.
That's why you're stupid.
'Fuck me, I don't want to die.'
*No*body wants to die.

Nick I always loved your body.

Ruth . . . only madmen.
Sorry, lunatics.
Oh, yeah, yeah, yeah. Oh, Christ.
You don't know anything.
You only hurt yourself.
Your *own* self.

Pause.

Nick I'm sorry that I hurt you.

Ruth No. You are a ghoul.
You never know what's going on.

Nick I'm sorry. Ruth.

Ruth I'm *bleeding!*
Why do you do this? (*Pause.*) That you want to kill me.
Do you know? (*Pause.*) Do you know? (*She goes over and grabs him, and shakes him.*)

Nick I hit you.

Ruth Why? *Why?*

Nick I was frightened.

Ruth Of what? Tell me. I am not a *witch*. I do not *know*. You have to *tell* me. *Why?*

Nick I thought.

Ruth What?

Nick All my life.

Ruth What?

Nick All my life I thought that I would *meet* a person.
She . . .

Ruth What?

Nick She would say, 'Let us be lovers.' (*Pause.*)
She'd ask me.
'I know who you are.' (*Pause.*)
'I know you.'
'I know what you need.'
'I want to have your children.' (*Pause.*)
'I understand you.'
'I know what you are.'

Ruth (*to self, very softly*) Oh, God.

Nick I would fall down. I would fall down and thank God.
I'd thank God for my life.
I'd kiss the Earth.

Ruth You read too many books.

Nick We'd sit here in the winter and we'd talk and watch the snow.
And we would think things.

Ruth (*to self*) We could have sat here.

Nick And I feel these things.

Ruth (*to self*) . . . we could have.

Nick They confuse me.

Pause.

Ruth Yes. (*She starts to go in.*)

Nick Where are you going?

Ruth Well, I have to change my clothes. I'm wet.

Nick It all gets cold so fast. What is the point?

Ruth Will you get dressed – because you have to drive me to the bus?

Nick No. You should stay with me.

Ruth No. I cannot. I have to go.

Nick What is the point? No.
No. What is the point? If one is like the other?

Pause.

Where is your friendship in that?

Pause.

You made the bracelet. It says you will always love me.
(*Pause.*) You had it made.
No. You don't have to go.
I don't believe that.

Pause.

Why do you have to go?

Ruth You do not love me.

Nick How do you know?

Ruth Nicky . . .

Nick No. Please. No. Please stay with me.

Ruth I wish I could.

Nick But no. You can. You must stay.
I can't sleep alone, you know that.
I can't sleep when I am by myself. I have these dreams . . .
you know that . . .

Ruth Nick . . .

Nick I don't feel good.
I am inside this hole.

Ruth Come back inside.

Nick No.

Ruth Yes. Before it starts to rain.

Nick Stay with me.

Ruth No.

Nick I sit here. Wait. I sit here. It gets dark. I cannot read. I
need you to be up here. (*Pause.*) I need time. Do you hear me?
I need time. Down in the City everything is vicious. I need
time to be up here. (*Pause.*) Everything is filthy down there.
You know that. I come up here, I see things. (*Pause.*) I cannot
sleep. I have these dreams at night. I dream. No, wait. I'll
tell you. (*Pause.*) I see the window, and the shades are
blowing. There has come a breeze, and all the curtains blow.
They are on fire.
It laps around the window. On all sides.
Someone is calling my name. Nicholas.
I swear to you.
I hear them in a voice unlike a man or woman. When I look,
I do not want to know. I know that there is something there.
I look. I see a bear. A bear has come back. At the window. Do
you hear me, Ruth?
Do you know what this *is*? To crawl beneath my house.
This house is *mine* now. In its hole it calls me.
In the Earth. (*Pause.*) Nicholas.
He's standing upright. On his legs. He has a huge erection. I
am singed. He speaks a human language, Ruth. I know. He

has these thoughts and they are trapped inside his mouth.
His jaw cannot move. He has thoughts and feelings, BUT
HE CANNOT SPEAK.
If only he could *speak*.
If only he could say the thing he wants.

Ruth What does he want?

Nick I DO NOT KNOW!

Ruth No! (*She hits him.*)

Pause.

Nick It smells like fish up here.

She hits him again.

Ruth You speak to me.

Nick You know I cannot speak.
I'm falling.

Ruth No.

Nick I'm falling in a hole.

Ruth There is no hole.

Nick There is. I do not like the way it smells.

Ruth You stop this.

Nick I have seen it all come back.

Ruth You stop this.

Nick I don't want to die. Oh, God. I do not want to die. I
am insane. Am I insane? I knocked you off the porch. I hurt
you. (*Pause.*) I feel like things are swimming. Ruth. Am I
insane?

Ruth No.

Nick Yes. I am. How can I live like this? I tried to kill you.

Ruth No. You didn't.

Nick Yes. You know I wanted to. I can't control myself.
I'm going swimming. (*He starts off the porch.*)

Ruth Sit down.

Nick No. I'm going in the water.

Ruth You sit down.

Nick I cannot live like this. I'm sorry.

Ruth You aren't going anywhere. There's nothing wrong with you.

Nick There is.

Ruth *hits him.*

Ruth You *shit*. You stupid *shit*. You sit down and don't *move*.
You are *alright*. You are alright. (*She hits him again.*)
Can't you *hear* me?
Are you *deaf*?
You are alright. There's nothing wrong with you.

Nick I'm going under. (*He starts to get up.*)

Ruth No. You are not. (*She stops him.*)

Nick Oh, yes. (*Screaming.*) What are we *doing* here?
What are we *doing* here?

Pause.

What will *happen* to us? *We* can't know ourselves.
. . . How can we *know* ourselves?
I have to leave.

Ruth You stop this. I will kill you before you will leave this
porch alive.

Nick I'm going under. (*He starts to go.*)

Ruth No. I *will*. (*Attacking him.*) I *will*. You *stop*! (*She hits him
in the face several times. Softer.*) You stop.

Pause. He is subdued. They both are on the floor.

Nicky.

A long pause.

Nick My face hurts.

Ruth You are just afraid.

Pause.

Nick No.

Ruth You are alright.

Nick I don't think that I am.

Ruth I swear to you. You listen to me.
I swear on my life. You are alright now.

Pause.

You are alright.

Nick Hold on to me.

Ruth Yes. (*She does so.*)

Nick I feel strange.

Ruth Yes. Tell me. Tell me.

Nick Wait. I have to talk to you. I have to tell you
something. Wait.

Pause.

We would come up here . . .

Pause.

I have to tell you we would come up here as children.
(*Pause.*) Although some things would happen.

Ruth Yes. Yes.

Nick But they were alright.

Ruth (*to self*) In the end.

Pause.

Nick Although we were frightened.

Ruth Yes.

Nick And many times we'd come up with a friend.
With friends. We'd ask them here. (*Pause.*)
Because we wanted to be with them.
(*Pause.*) Because . . . (*Pause.*) Wait.
Because we loved them.

Ruth I know.

Pause.

Nick Oh, my God. (*Pause. He starts to cry.*)
I love you, Ruth.

Pause.

Ruth No.

Nick I do, I love you, Ruth.

Pause.

Ruth Thank you.

Pause.

Nick I love you.

Ruth No.

Nick Yes. (*Pause.*)
Oh, God, I'm tired.

Ruth I know.

Nick Can you stay with me?

Ruth Come here.
Shhhh.

Nick Can you stay with me?

Ruth It's going to be alright.

Nick Please talk to me.

Ruth It's going to be alright.

Nick (*pause*) Will you talk to me?

Ruth What shall I say?

Nick Just talk to me.
I think I'm going to go to sleep.

Ruth You go to sleep now.

Nick Yes. I have to hear your voice.

Ruth Alright.

Nick I am so sleepy.

Ruth Shhhh. (*Pause.*)
Shhhh
There were two children . . .
Go to sleep. It's alright.
Go to sleep now.
They went for a walk.
Into the Forest. (*Pause.*)
Their Granma told them not to go too far.
Or else they might get lost.
For you must all be careful when you go into the woods.
And they went in.
It started to get dark.
He said he thought that they had lost their way.

Nick Are you alright?

Ruth Yes.

Nick Are you cold?

Ruth No.
They lay down.

Pause.

He puts his arm around her.

Pause.

They lay down in the Forest and they put their arms around
each other.
In the dark. And fell asleep.

Pause.

Nick Go on.

Pause.

Ruth What?

Nick Go on.

Ruth (*to self*) Go on . . .

Nick Yes.

Pause.

Ruth The next day . . .

The lights fade.

Lakeboat

This play is dedicated to John Dillon and to Larry Shue.

Lakeboat was first staged by the Theatre Workshop at
Marlboro College, Marlboro, Vermont, in 1970. It then sat
in my trunk until John Dillon, Artistic Director of the
Milwaukee Rep, discovered it in 1979.

John worked with me on the script, paring, arranging, and
buttressing; and its present form is, in large part, thanks to
him. I would also like to thank him and the men and women
of the Milwaukee Rep – actors, designers, and crew – for
their beautiful production of the play.

The Characters:

Pierman, *thirties or forties*
Dale, *Ordinary Seaman. Twenty*
Fireman, *Engine. Sixties*
Stan, *Able-Bodied Seaman. Deck. Forties*
Joe, *Able-Bodied Seaman. Deck. Forty or fifty*
Collins, *Second Mate. Thirties or forties*
Skippy, *First Mate. Late fifties*
Fred, *Able-Bodied Seaman. Deck. Thirties or forties*

Setting:

The Lakeboat *T. Harrison*. The engine room, the galley, the fantail (the farthest aft part of the ship), the boat deck, the rail.

The set, I think, should be a *construction* of a Lakeboat, so that all playing areas can be seen at once, no scenery needs to be shifted, and the actors can simply walk from one area to the next as their scenes require.

Lakeboat was first produced by the Court Street Theater, a project of the Milwaukee Repertory Theater, Milwaukee, Wisconsin, 24 April 1980, and the following cast:

Pierman	Gregory Leach
Dale	Thomas Hewitt
Fireman	Paul Meacham
Stan	Eugene J. Anthony
Joe	Larry Shue
Collins	John P. Connolly
Skippy	Robert Clites
Fred	Victor Raider-Wexler

Directed by John Dillon
Settings by Laura Maurer
Lighting by Rachel Budin
Costumes by Colleen Muscha
Properties by Sandy Struth
Stage manager Marcia Orbison

Scenes

Scene 1

What Do You Do with a Drunken Sailor?

The Lakeboat is being offloaded. **Dale** *talks with the* **Pierman**, *who is supervising the offloading.*

Pierman Did you hear about Skippy and the new kid?

Dale What new kid?

Pierman Night cook. Whatsisname that got mugged?

Dale No. What happened?

Pierman Well, you know, this new kid is on the beach . . .

Dale Yeah . . .

Pierman And, how it happened, he's in East Chicago after the last pay draw . . .

Dale Yeah . . .

Pierman . . . last week and drawed all he could and he's making the bars with a C or so in his pocket and flashing the wad every chance he gets . . .

Dale Oh boy.

Pierman What does the kid know? What do they know at that age, no offense.

Dale Yeah.

Pierman And, as I understand it, this slut comes on to him, and they leave the bar and he gets rolled.

Dale By the whore?

Pierman Yeah, I mean he'd had a few . . .

Dale The bitch.

Pierman . . . and wasn't in any shape. Anyway she takes his wad and his Z card.

Dale Not his Z card?

Pierman Yep and his gate pass . . .

Dale And he didn't even get laid . . . did he?

Pierman Fuck no, she rolled him first. Then she left.

Dale Bitch.

Pierman So, he stumbles back to the gate, drunk and sobbing . . .

Dale Nothing to be ashamed of . . .

Pierman The guards won't let him in! I mean he's bleeding, he's dirty . . .

Dale You didn't tell me he was bleeding.

Pierman It was understood . . .

Dale So, go on.

Pierman And dirty, and no identification. So, of course, they won't let him in.

Dale Bastards.

Pierman Yeah, well, they're just doing their job.

Dale I suppose you're right.

Pierman Pretty nice guys, actually.

Dale I suppose.

Pierman And so . . . where was I?

Dale The part where they won't let him in.

Pierman And so the guards won't let him in. But, uh . . . whatsisname, guy about thirty, so, you know him?

Dale I'm new.

Pierman Well, whatsisname happens to be coming through and of course he recognizes . . . whatsisname.

Dale Yeah.

Pierman So, 'What happened? Are you alright?' . . . all that shit. And the guard explains to him how they can't let the guy through and the guy vouches right up for him.

Dale He's a good man, huh?

Pierman And they *still* won't let him through.

Dale Yeah.

Pierman So, how he got *in* . . .

Dale Yeah.

Pierman He waited until these guards are looking the other way . . .

Dale Yeah.

Pierman . . . at a secretary or a train, I don't know. And they walked right through the main gate.

Dale Bunch of assholes, huh?

Pierman Well, I don't know . . . So, what happened with Skippy . . . you know Skippy?

Dale No.

Pierman The First Mate.

Pause.

Dale Oh yeah.

Pierman So what happened with him is this: The poor slob gets back to the fucking boat – drunk and bleeding and broke, right?

Dale Poor sonofabitch.

Pierman He gets to the gangway and the Second is on deck supervising offloading.

Dale Right.

Pierman Talking on the box with Skippy, the First Mate, who is up in the bridge. Now, Skippy sees this poor thing tromping up the pier and he says to Collins, the Second,

'Collins, we got passengers this trip,' which they did, 'Get that man below and tell him to stay there until he's sober.'

Dale Huh.

Pierman Although he is a hell of a nice guy, Skippy. Oldest First Mate on the Lakes. Did you know that?

Dale No.

Pierman Was a Master once. I don't know who for. That's why they call him Skippy.

Dale How do you know that?

Pierman I heard it. I don't actually know it. But that's why they call him Skippy. And so, anyway, Collins collars the slob and tells him to get below. 'Who says so?' the guy says. 'The First says so,' Collins says. Guigliani, Guilini, something like that.

Dale What?

Pierman The guy's name. So anyway. Guigliani, whatsisname, says, 'Tell the First to go fuck himself.'

Dale Oh, Christ.

Pierman So, as God would have it, at that precise moment the box rings and it's Skippy wanting to talk to Collins. 'Collins,' he says, 'What's holding up the Number Three Hold?' 'I'm talking to Guliami,' says Collins. 'What the all-fired fuck does he have to say that is so important?' says Skippy. 'He's telling me I should tell you to go fuck yourself . . .' says Collins. So Skippy, who bandied enough words at this point, says, 'Collins, throw that man in the canal and get Three Hold the fuck offloaded,' which I was working on, too, at that point.

Dale So?

Pierman So what?

Dale So did he throw him in the canal?

Pierman I don't know, I was below. I *heard* this.

Pause.

Dale And where is the guy now?

Pierman What am I, a mindreader? On the beach somewhere, lost his job. Up in East Chicago, I guess.

Dale Poor sonofabitch.

Pierman Oh, I don't know.

*The **Pierman** goes on board the boat.*

Scene 2

Opening

Dale *talks to the audience.* **Stan** *is on the boat. The* **Fireman** *comes up the gangplank, followed by* **Joe**.

Dale (*to audience*) That's the Lakeboat. Built 1938 for Czerwiecki Steel. Christened *Joseph Czerwiecki*. Sold to Harrison Steel, East Chicago, Indiana, 1954, renamed *T. Harrison*. Length overall 615 feet. Depth 321 feet. Keel 586 feet. Beam 60. The floating home of 45 men.

Fireman Guigliani got mugged.

Dale I'm his replacement. Gross tons 8,225. Capacity in tons 11,406. A fair-sized boat. A small world . . .

Fireman So I've heard.

Joe *comes on board.*

Stan Yo, Joe.

Joe Hiya.

Dale . . . *T. Harrison*. A steel bulk-freight turbine steamer registered in the Iron Ore Trade.

Stan You pick up those razor blades?

Joe Shit. I fucking forgot, I'm sorry.

Scene 3

Drink

A conversation on the fantail. **Stan** *and* **Joe** *are killing time while the boat is at the pier.*

Stan   Boy was I drunk last night.

Joe   I'm still drunk.

Stan   That wine. Drink wine and it dehydrates you. When you drink water the next morning it activates the alcohol.

Joe   I'm so hung over I can't see.

Stan   Can't see, I can't even talk.

Joe   I can't even fucking think straight.

Stan   You couldn't think straight last night.

Joe   I was drunk last night.

Stan   You're still drunk.

Joe   Yep.

Stan   No good, man.

Joe   Yep.

Stan   No damn good.

Joe   Sure not.

Stan   No fucking good.

Joe   What? . . . Drinking?

Stan   Drinking, life, women, the Boat. No good.

Joe   It's not that bad.

Stan   No fuckin' good.

Joe   You been drinking?

Stan   Drinking? Don't talk to me about drinking. What the hell did it ever get me? Drinking? I was drinking before you were wiping your own ass. Beer? I've drunk more beer in my time than I can remember. I could tick off my life in beer caps. Bottles, cans, pop-tops, screw-tops, bottles . . . every man on the ship had his own opener.

Joe I remember.

Stan Around the neck. Holy Mary. Don't tell me about beer, Joe. Please don't tell me about beer. Domestic and imported. Beer? I've drunk beer . . . Wine!

Joe Ah, wine.

Stan Used to drink it with every meal. White, cherry. Love the stuff. You need a taste for wine.

Joe I've got one.

Stan Domestic and imported.

Joe I love the stuff.

Stan Red and *white*. I've drunk it. Wine with my food, cigarettes smoldering and chilled wine. Wine with fruit. Warmed, spice wine. Sweet cherry wine. I know wine, Joe.

Joe What about liquors?

Stan What about them?

Joe Yeah.

Stan For faggots. But booze . . .

Joe Booze!

Stan Scotch and rye. Drink bourbon by the fifty. When I lived at home? Drink? My father could drink.

Joe My father could, too.

Stan I say that man could put it *away*. A fifth a day and more, Joe, and *more*.

Joe My father, too.

Stan He loved the stuff.

Joe It killed him, my father.

Stan Drink it by the fifth. He never lacked for booze, that man. That's one thing I can say for him.

Joe Yeah.

Stan Nothing too good for him.

Joe Yeah.

Stan The old fart'd drink Sterno. He didn't give a shit.

Joe I know.

Stan That man could *drink*.

Joe What about your mother?

Stan She could drink, too.

Joe My mother couldn't drink.

Stan No?

Joe Old man said it was bad for her.

Stan What do they know of booze, the cunts?

Joe Nothing.

Stan They can't drink. You ever know a woman who could drink?

Joe Yeah.

Stan What do they know?

Joe A girl in Duluth.

Stan They don't understand it. It's a man's thing, drinking. A curse and an elevation. Makes you an angel. A booze-ridden angel. Drinking? I know my alcohol, boyo. I know it and you know I know it. And I know it.

Joe I'll take you below. I gotta go on watch.

Stan Domestic and imported.

Joe Come on, Stan.

Stan Any way you call it.

Joe I gotta go on watch.

Stan Mixed drinks? I know my mixed drinks. You name one, I know it. Mixed drinks.

Joe . . . Manhattan.

Stan I know it.

Joe Come on, Stan.

Stan Ah, leave me alone.

Joe Come on, I gotta go on watch.

Stan So go on watch, you fucking Polack.

Joe Who's a Polack?

Stan Trust a Polack . . . to go on watch . . . when I'm pissed.

Joe I'll take you down to the dunnage room and get you some coffee.

Stan Don't want any coffee. Want to go to sleep.

Joe Well, let's go, then.

Stan I want to sleep by myself.

Joe Okay, Stan, let's get you off your feet.

Stan Offa deck.

Joe Sure.

Stan And who are you to tell me to get off the deck of a ship we both happen to be on?

Joe Come on, goddamnit.

Stan Getting mad, huh?

Joe Stosh.

Stan Getting a trifle warm. Aren't you getting warm?

Joe Okay, Stan.

Stan Fucking no-class Polack.

Joe Okay, Stan.

Stan Can't even hold your liquor.

Joe *walks off.*

Scene 4

Offloading

Joe *wanders into the galley.* **Collins** *finds him there and puts him to work.*

Collins Litko!

Joe Yo!

Collins Skippy wants a sandwich.

Joe . . . I just came on.

Collins Get him a sandwich, will you?

Joe I just came *on* . . .

Collins It'll take you a minute.

Joe Uh.

Collins *Huh?*

Joe What about the nightman?

Collins He got mugged.

Joe Yeah? By who?

Collins Now, how the fuck should I know?

Joe You got a cigarette?

Pause.

Collins Yeah.

Joe Thanks.

Pierman *enters galley.*

Pierman Hot.

Collins Can we speed this up at all?

Pierman You'll be out by about two.

Collins You think?

Pierman Two, three. Got time for a cup?

Collins Yeah. Joe, go see what kind of sandwich Skippy wants, huh?

Joe Yeah. (*Exits.*)

Pierman Any chance of something to eat?

Collins Lost the nightman.

Pierman Oh yeah . . . Sorry.

Collins (*pause*) Cook's up the street. (*Pause.*) You want some pie?

Pierman Yeah.

Collins Any special kind?

Pierman Yeah, blueberry. What you got?

Collins We got some.

Pierman It's a bitch in here.

Collins Yeah.

Pierman Cooler on the dock.

Collins Yeah.

Pierman What's the next trip, Arthur?

Collins Duluth.

Pierman Yeah? Cool up there.

Joe *enters.*

Collins (*to* **Joe**) What'd he want?

Joe Egg on white bread.

Pierman Any guys on break out there, you notice?

Joe I didn't notice.

Pierman Uh.

Joe I was thinking about my sandwich. We gonna have a new nightman, Mr Collins?

Collins Huh?

Joe Nightman.

Collins Yeah, sure. Crender said we'll have him this trip.

Joe That's good. I don't want to make these sandwiches all the way to Canada. If you know what I mean. Not that I mind it. I just fucking hate making sandwiches. For other people to eat.

Collins Don't worry.

Joe I don't mind cooking for myself, though.

Collins Wrap it in wax paper, will you?

Joe Yeah, sure.

Collins (*leaving the galley*) And make sure you get those boats clean today, huh?

Joe Right as rain.

Scene 5

Fire and Evacuation Drills

Skippy, *making a tour of the boat, runs into* **Dale**.

Skippy That's right, assholes. Fuck off on your fire and evacuation drills and your ass is going to be in a big sling when we have to drill for the Coast Guard. You!

Dale Yes sir.

Skippy What's your number?

Dale What number, sir?

Skippy F and E. (*Pause.*) F and E, boy –

Dale I don't know what that means, sir.

Skippy Fire. Fire and evacuation.

Dale I . . . don't think I have one.

Skippy How long have you been on this ship?

Dale About three minutes, sir.

Skippy Yeah. Well, check out your fire and evacuation number, for God's sake, will you? Your F and E number, will you?

Dale Yessir. Who do I check it out with?

Skippy I do not know. Ask Joe Litko. You know him?

Dale I can find him, sir.

Skippy Good for you. Well, find him and listen hard.

Dale Yessir.

Skippy Bunch of children.

Scene 6

The Illusion of Motion

Skippy *continues back to the bridge, where he finds* **Collins**.

Skippy Where's my sandwich?

Collins Litko's getting it.

Skippy He's not in Stewards. Where's the nightman?

Collins Got mugged. He's in the hospital.

Skippy What's the number in Stewards?

Collins 2–3.

Skippy Call for me on that sandwich.

Collins (*on the intercom*) Stewards? Collins calling on that sandwich for Skippy. Well, who is there? Where's Litko? Well, get him.

Pause.

This is Collins, Second . . . (*To* **Skippy**.) they hung up. (*He spies* **Joe** *on the deck*.) There's Litko. LITKO! GO PICK UP THE DECK PHONE. NO! DON'T COME HERE. PICK UP THE PHONE.

Stan *and* **Fred** *passing by*.

Stan This boat is becoming a bureaucracy.

Fred Tell me.

They continue off. Phone rings.

Collins (*into phone*) Bridge, Collins. Litko, I've been trying to get you. What the fuck happened on Skippy's egg? Where have you been? Boatdeck? What about that sandwich. (*To* **Skippy**.) New nightman showed up.

Skippy Book him. Forget Litko.

Collins (*into phone*) Litko, forget it. Go back to the boats. Yeah. No. Forget it. (*He hangs up.*)

Skippy What's he doing on the boatdeck?

Collins Raeding.

Skippy What's he reading? See if you can find out.

Stan *and* **Fred** *stroll off.*

Stan (*to* **Fred**) Who was the most grotesque girl you ever fucked?

Fred I'd have to think about that.

Skippy I'd like to know.

Scene 7

The New Man

Collins *returns to the galley and encounters* **Dale**.

Collins You the new man?

Dale I guess.

Collins You're going to be the new nightman. Night-cook. You ever cooked before?

Dale No, a little.

Collins Well, we're going to book you nightman, what's your name?

Dale Katzman, Dale.

Collins Alright. We're going to book you. Then you're off until 10 p.m. tonight. You work ten till six-thirty straight shift. Half-hour for lunch. Your work should take you about four, five hours.

Phone rings

Get that.

Dale Hello, kitchen. Wait a minute. He wants the Mate.

Collins Gimme that. Collins. Yo. They're off. He got mugged. We got one. What kind? Fuck you. Okay. (*To* **Dale**.) You know how to make a sandwich?

Dale Sure.

Collins Make one for the First. The First Mate. And then make one for the Fireman.

Dale Right. What kind?

Collins For the First, an egg . . . and for the Fireman, how the fuck should I know? Make him an egg. Alright?

Dale Sure.

Collins Good.

Scene 8

Woploving

The **Fireman**, **Joe**, *and* **Stan** *are shooting the breeze in the engine room.*

Fireman So, the way I hear it: she told him she was divorced. How about that.

Joe So what?

Fireman I'm divorced.

Joe Sorry.

Fireman So they started to get really blind.

Joe My mother is blind.

Pause.

Fireman And could he spare her some change, twenty for the kids, a saw for some groceries, you know.

Joe Yeah.

Fireman And all of the time she's drinking this rum with coke and lime.

Joe Coke *and* lime?

Fireman That's what I heard.

Joe That's how they drink it in Italy.

Fireman You never been to Italy.

Joe Now how the FUCK do you know?

Fireman I . . .

Joe How the everlasting cocksucking FUCK do you know I never been to Italy?

Fireman Jesus.

Joe Don't do shit all day and tells me where I never been. (*Exits.*)

Fireman (*to* **Stan**) So, Collins tells me, she'd have a drink . . .

Stan Yeah.

Fireman He'd have a drink.

Stan Yeah.

Fireman But pretty soon he's getting up knocking over tables and he's staggering ready to die and she's walking in a straight line. Say, I wonder what's the matter with Joe?

Stan Why do you say something's the matter with him?

Fireman I only . . .

Stan Who the hell are you?

Fireman I only meant . . .

Stan Twenty-some years on the boats watching a little dial and you know about what's 'wrong with Joe?'

Fireman Lookit . . .

Stan Just listen to me. The man has done more shit in his life than you'll ever *forget*.

Fireman I only said . . .

Stan Just remember that, Mr Wiseass. He's been more places in his life than you *ever* been.

Fireman He's never been to Italy.

Stan What kind of woploving bullshit is that?

Fireman *I'm* fucking Italian, don't talk to *me*, Fred.

Dale (*enters the engine room; generally*) Hi.

Stan Hi.

Pause.

Dale How are you?

Stan Fine.

Dale That's good.

Stan In the sense that I feel like shit. Been to Italy. (*He exits.*)

Dale You want a sandwich?

Fireman Yeah. You the new nightman?

Dale Yes. Do you like egg?

Fireman I don't give a fuck.

Scene 9

Gauges

Dale What do you do down here?

Fireman Down here? I read.

Dale How can you read and do your job?

Fireman I'm not answerable to you. I'm answerable to the Chief.

Dale I was just asking.

Fireman I do my job okay.

Dale I know that.

Fireman I do it okay. I keep busy . . . I read a bit . . .

Dale It doesn't get in your way, the reading?

Fireman Nooo. I mean, I gotta watch the two gauges. Four actually. We got the two main, they're the two you gotta watch, and the two auxiliary.

Dale Uh huh.

Fireman But you gotta keep your eye on those two main, because if they go, well . . .

Dale *Oh*, yeah.

Fireman I mean if that main goes, if she goes redline, you're fucking fucked.

Dale You switch over to the auxiliary?

Fireman I don't do nothing! I don't do a damn nothing. I'm not supposed to touch a thing. I shut down whichever blows, larboard or starboard. I shut down and I call the bridge and I call in the Chief, in that order.

Dale And then you watch the auxiliary?

Fireman Nothing to watch. The engine's shut down and the gauges is dead.

Dale Well, what's the point of having an auxiliary gauge?

Fireman For a standby. You gotta have a standby . . .

Dale Oh.

Fireman You don't have a standby, with that automatic oil feed! You don't have a standby and the main goes, you're fucking *fucked*. You know what I mean.

Dale Oh yeah.

Pause.

And you keep an eye on them, huh?

Fireman What do you mean, 'keep an eye on them'? I'm watching 'em constantly. That's my job.

Dale I see that.

Fireman Of course, I read a *bit*. I mean, when you get down to it. What is there to do? Watching two gauges for four hours a clip?

Dale Uh huh.

Fireman That's eight hours a day watching two gauges. If you don't read, do something, you'd go insane.

Scene 10

No Pussy

Dale *climbs up out of the engine room and is accosted by* **Fred.**

Fred You the new man?

Dale Yep. Dale. Dale Katzman.

Fred Jewish, huh?

Dale Yeah.

Fred No offense.

Dale Thanks.

Pause.

Fred Well, Dale . . . coming on like this out of nowhere you got a thing or two to find out. Now, the main thing about the boats, other than their primary importance in the Steel Industry, is that you don't get any pussy. You got that?

Dale Yes.

Fred Except when we tie up. This is important to know because it precludes your whole life on the boats. This is why everyone says 'fuck' all the time.

Dale Why?

Fred They say 'fuck' in direct proportion to how bored they are. Huh?

Dale Yeah.

Fred Now, from the prospect of not getting any . . . you know about sex?

Dale I know it all.

Fred I see you mean that facetiously.

Dale Yeah.

Fred Because there sure is a hell of a lot to find out. I'm not going to offend you, am I?

Dale I don't know.

Fred Okay.

Pause.

You know, I didn't find out about sex until late in life, judging from my age of puberty, you gotta go on watch?

Dale Not until ten.

Fred . . . which came quite early, who can say why? Huh?

Dale Yeah.

Fred Around eight. What did I know then, right? Stroke books, jacking off with a few choice friends, you know. Am I right?

Dale You're right.

Fred For *years*. Until I'm in high school and I fall for this girl. Same old story, right? She's beautiful, she's smart, and I dig her. I take her out, right? So, times are different then (this was a few years ago) and after the movies we're dryhumping in the living room. The father is asleep upstairs, the mother is dead, same old story, right?

Dale Right.

Fred And all of a sudden the whole thing becomes clear to me. I mean in a flash all this horseshit about the Universe becomes clear to me, and I perceive meaning in life: I WANT TO FUCK. I want to stick it inside of her. Screw dryhumping. I want to get it wet. I want to become one with the ages of men and women before me down into eternity and goo in the muck from whence we sprung . . . you know what I mean?

Dale I know.

Fred And I'm on fire. I'm going OOOOOOOOOoh and AAAAAAAAAAAAaaah and like that and trying to undo her brassiere. (This girl had tits.) I don't even bother anymore. You know what I say? 'You do it,' I say. The joy is gone, you know? So, anyway. We're still humping and bumping and I'm trying to undo the brassiere and my knee, as if it had a mind of its own, and never a word spoken, had inserted itself between her legs and she's gyrating like crazy and saying . . . What do you think she is saying?

Dale 'I love you?'

Fred 'No,' she is saying, 'Oh, Fred, please don't.'

Dale So?

Fred So, like a dope, I don't. We look sheepish for a minute. She gets all straightened out and says she had a wonderful time, Freddy, and out I go. So, to make a long story short, after this happened another time, two times, I begin to get wise something is not as it should be. Also, I can't walk in the mornings. But my uncle, who is over, is conversing with me one night and, as men will do, we start talking about sex. He tells a story, I tell *my* story. This takes him aback. 'What?' he says. 'The way to get laid is to treat them like shit.' Now, you just stop for a moment and think on that. You've heard it before and you'll hear it again but there is more to it than meets the eye. Listen: THE WAY TO GET LAID IS TO TREAT THEM LIKE SHIT. Truer words have never been spoken. And this has been tested by better men than you or me. *So*, I thought it out a bit and decided to put it into action. I'm going out with Janice. Movies, walk home, couch, dryhumping, no . . . I hit her in the mouth. I don't mean slap, Dale, this is important. I mean hit. I fucking pasted her. She didn't know nothing. She is so surprised she didn't even bleed. Not a word did I speak, but off with her dress, panties, and my pants. I didn't wear any underwear. A lot of women find that attractive, did you know that?

Dale No.

Fred Well, I've only since found that out. Anyway. Smacko, spread the old chops and I humped the shit out of her. She's yelling: OOOOh. Don't, OOOOH, yesssssssss, OOOOooooh don't, Freddy. Yes, it's so gooooooooood, my father'll hear ooooooh. SHEEEEEEEEEEEEIT. Zingo. So I got dressed and she's lying there on the couch spent, I mean, spent and wet and everything. (She looked beautiful.) And I go over to the door. 'Not another word out of you, cunt,' I say. 'Ever.'

Dale What about her father?

Fred He was a boilermaker. So. After that it's handjobs in the assembly hall, fucking under the bleachers, the whole thing, man. She's buying presents and asking *me* to the prom (I'd left school). And to this day. I mean to this day, I want a piece, I call her up and tell her, not ask her, *tell* Daley, I tell her where and when, and she's there. And she's *married*. So remember . . . I know, I *know*, I was a shy kid *too*. But you gotta remember, the way to a woman's cunt is right through her cunt. That's the only way. *Fershtay*?

Dale Uh huh.

Fred Let's get something to eat.

Dale I gotta make up the First's cabin.

Fred Okay. I'm gonna see you later.

Joe *and* **Stan** *pass. Part of their conversation can be heard.*

Joe Guy can't take care of himself he oughta stay out of East Chicago. *Huh?*

Stan Yeah.

Pause.

Joe They aren't in business for their health . . .

Scene 11

Mugged

Fred, *alone by the rail, soliloquizes.*

Fred Mugged. Yeah. Poor son of bitch. In East Chicago. That's a lousy town. By some whore, no less. Drugged the shit out of him, I guess. Met her in a bar. Who knows. He was a fanatic, you know? I knew him. Not overly well, but I knew him. He was a gambling degenerate. Played the ponies. How did he do I don't know. But I had my suspicions that he gave it all away. So who knows. Maybe the Maf got him. I mean, somebody got him. Maybe the whore, huh? So maybe it's the Murphy man, but I don't think so. It looks like the Outfit. Not that they care for the few C's they took. But you know how they are. You can't get behind. When you're into them that's it. Am I right? No. It doesn't figure. Unless it was the Outfit. Or some freak occurrence. It was probably some Outfit guys got him. Assuming he was into them. It doesn't look like he just got rolled. Beat the living fuck out of him. Left him for dead. Huh? Can you feature it? Flies in his face. Fucking ear stuck to the sidewalk with blood. Ruptured man, he'll never perform again. Ribs, back. The *back*. Hit him in the back. Left him for *dead*.

Pause.

It doesn't figure. The only way it adds up, if it was the Outfit. A very property-oriented group. Poor sucker.

Scene 12

Fred Busted at the Track

Fred *wanders into the galley, where he meets* **Stan**.

Stan Boy, did I get laid last night.

Fred One of the guys on the boat?

Stan By a woman, Freddie, a woman. You remember them? Soft things with a hole in the middle.

Fred I remember them.

Stan You look down, Freddy.

Fred I am down.

Pause.

Why did they have to go and build a racetrack on the south side of Chicago?

Stan Somebody made a survey. What did you lose?

Fred Seven hundred bucks.

Stan Where'd you get seven hundred bucks?

Fred Around.

Stan Oh.

Pause.

You in trouble?

Fred No.

Stan You sure?

Fred Yeah.

Pause.

Stan You sure?

Fred Yeah. Thank you. Yeah.

Stan You'd tell me if you were?

Fred Yeah.

Pause.

Stan Okay you watch yourself. (*He leaves the galley.*)

Fred Thank you.

Scene 13

Fred on Horseracing

Fred *continues his soliloquy.*

Fred Because it's clean. The track is clean. It's like life
without all the complicating people. At the track there are
no two ways. There is win, place, show, and out-of-the-
money. You decide, you're set. I mean, how clean can you
get? Your bet is down and it's DOWN. And the winners
always pay. Something. Into the turn, backstretch, spinning
into the turn and heading for home. It's poetry. It's a
computer. You don't even have to look at the fucking things.
It's up on the board and it's final and there are two types of
people in the world.

Pause.

Next post in fifteen minutes.

Collins (*entering the galley*) The next post is up your ass if you
don't get to work.

Fred I'm gone.

Fred *leaves the galley and runs into* **Joe** *on the deck.*

Joe (*as if resuming a conversation*) . . . why I never got along
with women. I just had too much dynamite in me.

Fred . . . it happens . . .

They walk down the fantail.

Scene 14

Personal Sidearms

Skippy *and* **Collins** *are on the bridge.*

Skippy . . . the *Luger* was the enlisted man's sidearm, and the *Walther* was the officer's.

Collins Are you sure?

Skippy I was *there*, my friend. I was *there* . . .

Scene 15

The Cook Story

Joe *and* **Fred** *on the fantail.*

Fred I heard the cook has two Cadillac Eldorados.

Joe This year's?

Fred Last year. One in Chicago, Chicago Harbor, and the other in Arthur.

Joe How long's he been on the run?

Fred About twenty years, I guess.

Joe Yeah.

Fred More or less . . . ten, twenty years.

Joe What's he want with two Caddies?

Fred So's he can have one here and one there.

Joe So he can have one everywhere he goes.

Fred Yeah. Well, he's only got two. He's not married.

Joe That's it. That's the big difference. Right?

Fred You said it. That's the difference . . . between him . . .

Joe Yeah, that's it. Cocksucker can probably *afford* two cars.

Fred Oh, yeah. Well, he's got 'em.

Joe Cocksucker probably doesn't know what it *is* to be married.

Fred He was married once.

Joe Yeah?

Fred Yeah, I think. Yeah. He was married. I heard that.

Joe Where'd you hear it, on the Boat?

Fred Yeah. He used to be married. To a girl. She used to ship on the Boats.

Joe Yeah?

Fred Oh yeah, they used to ship Stewards together. They stopped. They got divorced.

Joe Bastard's probably forgot what it is to be married.

Pause.

Two cars.

Fred What the fuck? He worked for them.

Joe I'm not saying he didn't work for them.

Fred Oh no.

Joe I never said that, I mean, it's obvious he worked for them. He's got 'em, right?

Fred As far as I know.

Joe Well, has he got 'em or not?

Fred Yeah, he's got 'em . . . as far as I know.

Joe Probably only got a couple of Chevys.

Fred Yeah.

Joe A couple of '56 Chevys.

Fred Yeah.

Joe Cocksucker's only probably got a pair of used Volkswagens.

Fred I don't know . . .

Joe Or a beat-up Buick.

Fred Yeah.

Joe Or a fucking De*Soto* for Christ's sake. Who the fuck knows he's got two Caddies?

Fred Well, he's not married. I know that much.

Joe Lucky son of a bitch.

Fred It's a tough life.

Joe Oh yeah?

Fred Yeah. I was married once.

Joe Yeah?

Fred Yeah. I'm still married. To my second wife.

Joe You got divorced, huh?

Fred Why do you say that?

Joe You just said you're married to your second wife.

Fred Oh yeah. I got divorced . . . from my first.

Joe Yeah, I'm sorry. I mean, she could of died. You could of been a widower.

Fred It's too late now.

Joe You pay any alimony?

Fred Yeah, ho, shit, did I pay? I was doing extra deckwork and running to the track so that woman could fuck off and pamper the kids.

Joe How many kids you have?

Fred . . . just one, actually. I don't know why I said 'kids'.

Joe They live with their mother, huh?

Fred Yeah. Actually there's just one kid, Clarice. She's the kid.

Joe A girl, huh?

Fred Yeah. She lives with her mother.

Joe You see her?

Fred Oh yeah. What do you think? I just let her live with that cunt? Christ. I see her every chance I get. Her birthday . . . we go to the *zoo* . . . museums . . . She got married, my wife, ex.

Joe Well, shit. At least you don't have to pay alimony.

Fred Yeah. But doesn't she fuck me on the child support? Every fucking piece of kleenex has to come from Carson Pirie Scott. What fucking kid spends eighty dollars a month? What happens to eighty dollars a month? I'll tell you, Denise ex-fucking-Swoboda is what happens. Nothing is too good for the kid. But it takes a bite.

Joe What doesn't?

Fred That is a point, Joe. It's getting expensive just to live.

Joe Sure as shit.

Fred Just to buy a pack of Camels is getting you have to go to the fucking bank. Used to be twenty-six cents a pack in Indiana.

Joe I can remember it used to be seventeen cents in Tennessee.

Fred You aren't from there.

Joe We used to go there.

Fred Ah.

Joe (*pause*) I wish I never got started. I used to buy 'em for my old man. He used to say, 'You gotta smoke, don't hide it. Smoke in my presence.'

Fred So did you?

Joe Christ no, he woulda beat the shit outta me.

Fred You should never of gotten started. It's too fucking expensive. Fuck. Eighty-five cents.

Joe It's going up.

Fred Where is it going to stop? I swear to God I don't know. We'll all be selling syphilitic fucking apples to each other on the street corner.

Joe You give any money on Poppyseed days?

Fred No. They want loot, let 'em work on the ship.

Joe I always wanted to be a pirate. Ever since I was a little kid.

Fred . . . or digging ditches, though somebody's gotta run the ships, right?

Joe . . . yeah.

Fred I mean, the cook's gotta keep up his payments.

Joe That's a good one, alright.

Scene 16

Sidearms Continued

On the bridge.

Collins So what was the Walther Luger.

Skippy There was no such thing.

Collins I read it.

Skippy Where?

Collins In some book on the War.

Skippy Then you were lied to. There was no such thing. Believe me.

Pause.

Collins I *read* it.

Skippy No. I'd tell you if it were the case. (*Pause.*) I would. If it were the case.

Scene 17

Jonnie Fast

Fred *and* **Stan** *are smoking cigarettes on the boat deck.*

Fred I'm going to *tell* you: Jonnie Fast is the strongest guy in ten years.

Stan You know what? You are truly an idiot. You could of said that in the dark and I would of known it was you because only you could make so stupid a statement. Jonnie Fast has got to be the dumbest cocksucker I can remember.

Fred Yeah. That's like you to say that.

Stan You know about it . . . ?

Fred I know when a guy is strong.

Stan And that's what Fast is. Strong, huh?

Fred Yeah.

Stan You know. I agree with you one hundred percent. He is strong, this Fast. He's probably the strongest guy I've ever seen. I can't think of anything that would be stronger than he is. Unless maybe a pile of shit.

Fred What do you know. Who do you like?

Stan Oh . . . I'll tell you. You want a really *strong* fellow. A real type, I'd have to say . . . Jerry Lewis. He could probably knock the shit outta Fast.

Fred You don't know nothing. You don't know a champ when you're fucking looking at him at the movies, for chrissake. This guy is stark. He is the best.

Stan He's the best, alright. Like jacking off is better than getting laid. This guy Fast is the fucking jackoff of all time.

Fred Yeah. I see your point, Stan. I agree with you. The man is not stark. He's no fucking good. That's why he didn't take five fucking guys in that barroom using only one pool cue. I see your point.

Stan Shirley Temple probably couldn't've taken those guys, I suppose.

Fred Oh, no. Shirley Temple probably could've taken them. She could've disarmed them and probably shot that meat knife out've the guy's hand from twenty feet from the hip . . . yeah, I see your point.

Stan And I suppose this guy could whip the shit out've Clint Eastwood, huh? I really think that. Explain that to me, will you, Joe? How Clint Eastwood is no match for this guy?

Fred Oh, well . . .

Stan No, explain it to me.

Fred If you want to get ridiculous about it . . .

Stan Or Lee Van Cleef. I'm *sure*, he would've laid down and puked from fear when he saw this guy two blocks off.

Fred All I know is, like you say, any guy who fucks all night and drinks a shitload of champagne and can go out at five the next morning and rob a bank without a hitch has to be no fucking good. I see your point.

Stan 'No fucking good?' No! He's great! He only had the entire National Guard worth of sidekicks, about two thousand guys and an A-bomb to back him up. You really gotta admire a stand-up guy like that.

Fred He didn't have no bomb.

Stan Pardon me.

Fred Where do you get this 'bomb' shit? You probably didn't even see the movie, all you know.

Stan No, you're right. I probably didn't even see the movie. That's how come I don't know what a bustout Jonnie Fast is, and what a complete loser you are to back him. I probably never did see the picture. In fact, I've probably never been to a movie in my life and I'm not standing on a boat. And your name isn't Fred, I suppose. Oh, and you're probably not completely full of shit.

Fred Probably not.

Stan You idiot, what do you know.

Stan *walks off.*

Scene 18

The Inland Sea Around Us

Joe, *on the boat deck, is contemplating the lake.* **Collins**, *making his evening rounds, walks by.*

Joe Evening, Mr Collins.

Collins Joe.

Joe Mr Collins, how far is it to land out here?

Collins I don't know, about five miles.

Joe How long could a guy live out here, do you think?

Collins What?

Joe I mean, not if he was on an island or anything, or in a boat. I mean in the water. I mean . . . it's over your head.

Collins Don't really know, Joe. You planning a swim?

Joe Swim? Swim? Oh! I get you. A swim! Yeah, no. I was just wondering in case, God forbid, we should go down and the life-boats were all leaky or something. How long do you think a fellow would last?

Collins Joe . . .

Joe You can tell me.

Collins Don't worry about it, huh? Even if the boat sunk you've got jackets and they'd have a helicopter here in a half-hour.

Joe Oh, I don't worry about it. I just wonder. You know.

Collins Sure, Joe. Well, don't wonder.

Joe I guess the big problem wouldn't be the drowning as much as the boredom, huh?

Collins See you, Joe.

Joe Night, Mr Collins.

Scene 19

Arcana

Stan *and* **Joe** *walk across the fantail.*

Stan There are many things in this world, Joe, the true meaning of which we will never know. (*Pause.*) I knew a man was a Mason . . .

Joe Uh huh . . .

Stan You know what he told me?

Joe No.

Pause.

Stan Would you like to know?

Joe Yes.

As **Stan** *starts to speak, they continue around the fantail and out of sight.*

Scene 20

Dolomite

Collins *continues to the bridge.* **Skippy** *is in command of the ship.* **Collins** *philosophizes.*

Collins (*to* **Skippy**) You know, it's surprising what people will convince themselves is interesting. The Company, guests come on for a trip and we're docked at Port Arthur and they're up on the boatdeck and for an hour, an hour and a half, they're watching this stuff pour into the holds. Just watching it pour into the holds and the dust is flying and it's hard to breathe. But they're just standing there. The woman's got a Brownie. She's taking pictures of rock falling off a conveyor belt. Now what is so interesting about that? I'd like to know. If you described the situation to them, to any normal people, they wouldn't walk across the hall to watch it if the TV were broken. But there they are, guests of the Company. Standing there on the boatdeck hours on end, watching the rocks and the dust. Maybe they see something I don't. Maybe I'm getting jaded.

Pause.

What are they looking at?

Skippy What are *you* looking at? You're looking at them.

Collins That's perfectly correct.

Skippy It's all a matter of perspective. (*Pause.*) *Yes*sir.

Pause.

Scene 21

The Bridge

Skippy *is alone as* **Collins** *leaves the bridge.* **Joe** *and* **Dale** *are alone in the galley.*

Skippy (*on the radio*) W.A.Y., Chicago, this is the *T. Harrison*, Harrison Steel, en route. I am ready to copy. Over.

Joe What time you go off?

Dale Around six-thirty.

Joe Hit the bridge before then.

Dale Yeah.

Joe Hit it in about a half-hour.

Dale Yeah.

Joe Hit it about six. You made up the First's cabin yet?

Dale Yeah. I was up forward a little while ago. Going to be a nice day.

Joe Hot.

Dale You think?

Joe Yeah. Well, be hot when we tie up. Be hot before we hit the Soo. You going up the street?

Dale Oh, I don't know. Later maybe. Going to get some sleep first.

Joe They got some nice bars up there.

Dale Yeah?

Joe Oh yeah. I know. Got some real bars up there. Sedate . . . Yeah. I used to go up there. To go drinking up there.

Dale You off now?

Joe Naw. I don't go off till the eight o'clock come on. I don't go off till eight.

Dale You hungry?

Joe Yeah, a little.

Dale Want me to fix you something?

Joe Naw. I'll get me some pie, something. We got any pie left?

Dale Should be some. Want something to drink? A glass of milk?

Joe Naw, I'll just get some coffee. You know, Dale . . . you go to school?

Dale Yeah, I'm in my second year.

Joe You're starting your second year, you finished one year?

Dale Yeah. I'll be starting my sophomore year in September. When I go back.

Joe Where do you go at?

Dale In Massachusetts. Near Boston.

Joe What do you go all the way there for?

Dale Well, I like it there. It's a good school . . . It's a nice area.

Joe Yeah, but they got good schools over here, don't they? I mean, I'm sure it's a good place . . . where you go. But they got good schools here, too. Loyola, Chicago University, some good schools here . . . Michigan.

Dale Oh, yeah. They're good schools. But I like it in the East.

Joe It's nice there, huh?

Dale Yes, very nice. Nice country. I like it there.

Joe What are you studying, I mean, what do you work at, at school?

Dale I'm studying English. English Literature.

Joe Yeah? That's a tough racket. I mean, writing. But . . . what? Are you gonna teach? To teach English?

Dale Oh, I don't know. I'm just . . . studying it because I like it.

Joe Yeah.

Dale I may teach.

Joe Sure, I mean . . . all I mean, it's a tough racket, you know? . . . Hitting the bridge soon?

Dale Yup.

Joe How long will you be staying on the boat? About?

Dale Oh, I don't know. Another month, five weeks.

Joe Got to go back to school, back East, huh?

Dale Yeah. I'll leave to go back to school.

Joe Want a cup? . . . Going back to your studies. Back East. I used to go East. I worked out of Buffalo for a while. I shipped Ford out of Detroit, too. Ford Boats. Ever shipped salt?

Dale No, you?

Joe Never did. Always wanted to, though. It's a different life, you know?

Dale Yeah.

Joe It must be nice out there. Be pretty easy to ship out. Out of Chicago. I'm an A.B., did you know that? . . . You should get out of Stewards, you know? Get on the deck, get rid of this straightshift crap. If you were on the deck we could go up street at Duluth. Arthur. You'd be out, free, until four in the afternoon and you'd be free at eight and we could fuck around all night, you know? Really hit the bars.

Dale It's not so bad, really. I have my days free, I get some sun.

Joe Yeah, but it's not the same thing, it's like having a *job*, for crissakes. I mean, it's okay if you like it.

Dale It's alright.

Joe I been working on the Lakes off and on for twenty-three years. It don't seem like such a long time. How old are you, Dale, if you don't mind my asking?

Dale No, I'm eighteen. Be nineteen in October.

Joe Yeah? You're a young guy for such a . . . I mean, you're not that *young* but you seem . . . older, you know? You seem like you wouldn't of been that young. Of course, that's not that young. I was working on the boats before I was your age. I'm going to get some more pie . . . You can see the bridge. You can just make it out. Like a landmark out there. You know, that is one pretty bridge. We been going under that bridge for once or twice a week since I was your age off and on, but that sure is a pretty bridge.

Dale Yeah, I like it.

Joe But, I mean, what the fuck? It's a bridge, right? It's something that you use and takes cars from over there over to the island. They don't let no cars drive on that island, did you know that? It's a law. But what I mean, you usually do not think about things that way. From that standpoint. But when you look at it . . . it's just a bridge to get people from the island over to there on the beach . . . you know what I mean.

Dale Yeah.

Joe And . . . you go underneath of it and look up and all the same it's pretty. And you forget that it *does* something. But this beauty of it makes what it does all the more . . . nice. Do you know what I'm talking about?

Dale Yeah, Joe.

Joe Sometimes I get . . . well, I don't express myself too well, I guess.

Dale No, I know what you mean.

Joe You know, you got it made, Dale. You know that? You really got it made.

Dale What do you mean?

Joe You got your whole life ahead of you. I mean, you're not a *kid* or anything . . . you're a man. You're a young man. But you got it made.

Dale What are you talking about, Joe?

Joe Ah, you know what I'm saying.

Dale You're not an old man, Joe. What are you talking about?

Joe Ah, you know what I'm saying to you. I just wanted to tell you, Dale. I just wanted to let you know. So you'll understand. I mean. I've lived longer than you have. And at this stage one can see a lot of things in their proper light. And . . . you're a bright kid.

Dale Well, sometimes I don't think so.

Joe Well, what do you know? You know? I mean I've lived a hell of a lot longer than you have and I want to tell you, you're going to be Okay. You're a fine, good-looking kid and you know what's happening. You're okay and you're a good worker . . . I don't mean that disrespectfully.

Dale . . . I know.

Joe And I just want to tell you, sincerely, you have got it made.

Dale Well.

Joe No, it's the truth. Christ it's going to be hot today. Going to be a hell of a hot fucking day. Did you make up the First's cabin today?

Dale Before you came in.

Joe You don't have to take no shit from him, you know.

Dale I know that.

Joe He give you any trouble?

Dale No, not at all.

Joe Well, you don't have to take nothing from him. You just do your job. And if he gives you any trouble you talk to the Union Rep when we hit the beach. You know? You just do a good job . . . because that's what he's there for.

Dale Okay.

Joe I mean it. If he gives you shit, just let me know.

Dale Okay, Joe. I'll do that.

Joe Seriously. We should raise Mackinaw in a couple of minutes. You going up on deck?

Dale No, I gotta finish up here.

Joe Yeah, well, I'll see you later. Let me know if you're going up the street, huh?

Dale I will, Joe.

Joe We'll hit the bars.

Dale I will.

Joe You drink?

Pause.

Dale Yeah.

Joe Well, I'm going up on the boatdeck. You get off soon, huh?

Dale In about a half-hour.

Joe Well, take it easy, Dale. Get some rest. Can you sleep in this heat?

Dale Easy. I got a scoop out the porthole.

Joe Oh. Well, it's just that I have trouble sometimes. Well, take it easy, kid.

Dale Don't work too hard.

Joe Fuck no. I wouldn't.

Scene 22

Fast Examined

Stan, *on the main deck, buttonholes* **Collins**.

Stan . . . at least eight. But he doesn't ever draw his gun. He's giving 'em one of these (whack) and a couple of these, and some of these, twisting and like a ballet. Till there's one left. Behind the bar. And all you see: Jonnie's got his back to the bar. We think he thinks this guy is dead. And you see the guy take this cleaver off the bar and heft it over his head and just as he starts to let go, Fast whips around and fires. (Carries this belly pistol. Black as night. In his *sleeve*, in his fucking sleeve.) He goes whomp, like that and the fucking thing slides down his sleeve and into his hand. And you see the guy's still got his hand up to throw but all you see is this little bit of bloody handle. Fast shot the cleaver out of the guy's fucking hand. BEHIND HIS BACK. Twenty, thirty feet with a two-inch belly pistol. Now, how stark is that?

Scene 23

The .38

In the engine room.

Fireman . . . a big black Colt's revolver. A .38 or a .44.
Pure blue-black with a black checker grip and an eyelet on
the butt for a lanyard – it was an old gun, but in good shape.
No scratches. Purest black as a good pair of boots. Must've
been re-blued. Or maybe he never used it. You don't know.
Used big shells, powerful. You could tell from how big they
were. That's a good way to tell. I was in the Army. Overseas.
Hawaii. But it wasn't a state. The officers had pistols. They
were automatic. .45s. Big heavy things. But his was a
revolver. I've seen it. Shit, he used to take it down here to
clean it. He worked down here a while. Don't know how they
ever took him. A big guy as quick as he was. I don't see how.
Unless they drugged him – or took him from behind.

Fred I heard they might have drugged him.

Fireman Bastards.

Fred Or he was drunk.

Fireman Possible. Possible. Very possibly. That boy
drank. Used to drink on the ship.

Fred Who doesn't?

Fireman Not him, not him, for sure. No sir, stagger around
like an Indian when he had a few. Like a goddamn
Winnebago Indian he would.

Fred That's probably what happened. Did he have his gun
with him?

Fireman What'd you hear?

Fred Didn't hear one way or the other.

Fireman The way I hear it . . . he *took* it. He took the gun to
the bar . . . but when they *found* him. HE DIDN'T HAVE
IT ON HIM.

Fred Huh?

Fireman He was a mysterious fellow.

Fred Huh?

Fireman But he had a lot of gumption.

Fred I heard that, I didn't know him.

Fireman Yup, a lot of gall.

Fred Oh yeah.

Fireman I hated that . . . young fellow, what does he know? Blind balls is all. Damn fool like to get killed. Crazy. Crazy, is all. With a big gun like that.

Fred Maybe he didn't have it on him.

Fireman He had it. I think he had it, by God. I saw him going off and I said to myself, 'He looks like trouble. He just is dripping trouble today. I hope he's got his piece. I just hope, for his own sake that he's got it.'

Fred The cops would know if he had it.

Fireman Or someone could have looked in his stuff.

Fred They cleaned it out, huh?

Fireman Yeah, been cleaned out. I'd say, for sure. The Mate's responsible.

Fred Well, whether he took it or not, they got him.

Fireman Fucking cops.

Fred Yeah . . . why do you say 'cops'?

Fireman You kidding? It was the cops got him. Or Uncle Sam.

Fred The G? What'd the G want with Guiglialli?

Fireman You kidding? With what that kid knew?

Fred What'd he know?

Fireman Things. He knew things.

Fred Yeah?

Fireman Surer'n hell, that kid. He'd let on like he didn't know, but he knew. I know when they know. I can see it. And that kid's been around. The cops, they don't like that they find out, they don't sit still. They know. That kid was no cherry, either. He was no dumb kid. I think he was on the run. I think they wanted him.

Fred The Coast Guard wouldn't let him on the boats if he was wanted. They print you. You know that.

Fireman Still . . .

Fred How could he get on?

Fireman He had friends. That kid had friends, I tell you. Politics. Strings. You don't know one-half of what he knew. He was no cheap talker, that kid. Talk is cheap.

Fred You think it was the G, huh?

Fireman I think what I think. That's all I know.

Scene 24

Subterfuge

Dale *is at work in the galley.* **Joe** *comes in.*

Joe Hey, Dale. I heard the Steward's in charge of First Aid.

Dale What's the matter?

Joe It's just that I heard that. Is it the truth?

Dale Yup.

Joe Good. Good. I heard that. What I wanted to know and was wondering, out of curiosity, is: What happens if a guy gets his leg chopped off and they have to give him something? What do they give him?

Dale Morphine, I guess.

Joe They keep that stuff on the ship here?

Dale Not as far as I know. You'd have to ask the Steward.

Joe Oh, I wouldn't want to have to do that, because I'm just curious. I didn't really want to *know* or anything, you know?

Dale I understand.

Joe The Steward's the only one's got keys to First Aid, huh?

Dale Right.

Joe Well, alright. Thanks, you know.

Pause.

But would you do me a favor?

Dale Sure.

Joe Would you get me a couple of aspirins and a glass of water?

Dale Sure, Joe. You got a headache?

Joe Yeah. I'm not feeling so good the last couple of days.

Dale What is it?

Joe I don't know. My back down near my kidneys. It hurts. My head hurts all the time, you know?

Dale You think it's serious?

Joe I don't know. It just hurts. It makes you feel old, you know? Sometimes you just get so sick of everthing, nothing seems any good, you know? It's all you – don't care . . . Ahhh, it's just me being sick, is all.

Dale I thought you didn't look right today.

Joe My hair hurts.

Dale Mmmmm.

Joe And my kidney hurts when I walk – I think I'm dying.

Dale You don't look like you're dying, Joe.

Joe I sure as hell feel like I am. Sheeeeit.

Dale Just try to think it won't always be like this, Joe. It's just a temporary illness, in a day or two or a week it'll be all over.

Joe That's easy for you to say. You don't know what I got.

Dale What have you got?

Joe I don't know.

Dale Well. You can see a doctor the next time we tie up.

Joe Yeah. It kinda frightens me.

Dale It does?

Joe I don't wanna almost find out what I got.

Dale It's probably nothing serious, Joe. A virus, a little flu or some inflammation, you know?

Joe Or infection.

Dale A little infection isn't going to hurt you, Joe. It might only be a touch of stomach flu, something that's going to be over in a day or two. Have you had fever?

Joe Yeah. At night I been sweating out the sheets terrible. It's inhuman to sleep in them, you know? And I get cold, I don't know. I'm so fucking sick of being sick.

Dale How long has it been? Four or five days?

Joe Off and on, yeah, and longer than that.

Dale You should see a doctor, Joe.

Scene 25

Fingers

Joe *wanders off.* **Dale** *goes on deck for a cigarette and encounters* **Fred** *at work.*

Fred Collucci lost two fingers in the winch.

Dale Which winch?

Fred Forward main.

Dale Who's Collucci?

Fred Used to ship deck.

Dale When did he lose them?

Fred This was a couple, four – five years.

Dale Yeah.

Fred He got thirty-six hundred bucks.

Dale The Company paid him?

Fred Not counting Workman's Comp and Social Security.

Dale Do you get Social Security for fingers?

Fred I don't know. But not counting it he got thirty-six hundred bucks. Eighteen hundred bucks a finger.

Dale The main winch? Which fingers?

Fred Right hand. These two.

Dale That's a bitch. He's crippled.

Fred Two fingers?

Dale But the thumb.

Fred What about it, for thirty-six hundred?

Dale How could he pick anything up?

Fred Used the other fucking hand. If they paid him five bucks every time he wanted to pick something up just to use his left hand he'd get . . . thirty-six hundred bucks. . . . For 720 times . . . That's not so much.

Dale I wouldn't do it.

Fred He didn't do it on purpose.

Dale I wouldn't do it at all. Even by accident. No amount of money.

Fred I think.

Dale You can't buy a finger, man. It's gone and that's it. Not for all the money in the world.

Fred Yeah, neither would I.

Skippy and **Collins**, *on the bridge, are overheard.*

Skippy . . . explain it when we don't make schedule on this watch, you.

Collins I called ahead. They'll have the mail right at the lock.

Scene 26

Joe's Suicide

Dale, *off watch, is sharing a beer with* **Joe** *on the boatdeck.*

Joe You get paid for doing a job. You trade the work for money, am I right? Why is it any fucking less good than being a doctor, for example? That's one thing I never wanted to be, a doctor. I used to want to be lots of things when I was little. You know, like a kid. I wanted to be a ballplayer like everyone. And I wanted to be a cop, what does a kid know, right? And can I tell you something that I wanted to be? I know this is going to sound peculiar, but it was a pure desire on my part. One thing I wanted to be when I was little (I don't mean to be bragging now, or just saying it). If you were there you would have known, it was a pure desire on my part. I wanted to be a dancer. That's one thing I guard. Like you might guard the first time you got laid, or being in love with a girl. Or winning a bike at the movies . . . well, maybe not that. More like getting married, or winning a medal in the war. I wanted to be a dancer. Not tap, I mean a real ballet dancer. I know they're all fags, but I didn't think about it. I didn't *not* think about it. That is, I didn't say, 'I want to be a dancer but I do *not* want to be a fag.' It just wasn't important. I saw myself arriving at the theatre late doing *Swan Lake* at the Lyric Opera. With a coat with one of those old-time collars. (It was winter.) And on stage with a purple shirt and white tights catching these girls . . . beautiful light girls. Sweating. All my muscles are covered in sweat, you know? But it's clean. And my muscles all feel tight. Every fucking muscle in my body. Hundreds of them. Tight and working. And I'm standing up straight on stage with this kind of expression on my face waiting to catch this girl. I was about fifteen. It takes a hell of a lot of work to be a dancer. But a dancer doesn't even fucking care if he is somebody. He *is* somebody so much so it's not important. You know what I mean? Like these passengers we get. Guests of the Company. Always being important. If they're so fucking important, who gives a fuck? If they're really important why the fuck do they got to tell you about it?

Dale I remember in a journalism class in high school the teacher used to say, never use the word famous in a story. Like 'Mr X, famous young doctor . . .'

Joe Right, because if they're fucking famous, why do you have to say it?

Dale And he said if they're *not* . . .

Joe Then what the fuck are you saying it for, right?

Dale Right.

Joe It's so fucking obvious you could puke. No class cocksuckers. You ever try to . . . I don't want to get you offended by this, you don't have to answer it if you don't want to.

Dale No, go ahead.

Joe I mean, what the fuck? If you're going to talk to somebody, why fuck around the bush, right? Did you ever try to kill yourself?

Dale No.

Joe I did one time. I should say that perhaps I shouldn't say I 'tried' to kill myself, meaning the gun didn't work. But I wanted to.

Dale Yeah.

Joe I had this gun when I lived over on the south side. I won it in a poker game.

Dale Yeah.

Joe Aaaaaaah, I fucking bought it off the bumboat in
Duluth. Why lie? Forty bucks. A revolver. .32 revolver. Six
shots, you know?

Dale How big a barrel?

Joe A couple of inches. Like this. I never fired it. One time,
coming back, I loaded it and fired one shot off the fantail into
the water. I didn't hit anything. I used to clean it. Got this kit
in the mail. Patches and oil and gunslick and powder solvent
and this brush.

Dale I've seen them.

Joe I kept it in my suitcase. One night in Gary, I had this
apartment. I was cleaning my gun and, you know how you
do, pretending the cops were after me and doing fast draws in
the mirror.

Dale Yeah.

Joe And I said, 'What am I doing? A grown man playing
bang bang with a gun in some fucking dive in Gary Indiana
at ten o'clock at night?' And I lay down in front of the TV
and loaded the gun. Five chambers. You shouldn't load the
sixth in case you jiggle on your horse and blow your foot off.

Dale Yeah.

Joe And I put the end in my mouth, and I couldn't swallow
and I could feel my pulse start to beat and my balls contract
and draw up. You ever feel that?

Dale No.

Joe And I took it out of my mouth and laid down on the bed
on my back and looked at the ceiling and put the gun under
my chin pointing at my brain. But after a while I started
feeling really stupid. And I rolled over and put the gun under
my pillow, but I still held onto it. And I started. You know,
playing with myself, you know what I mean.

Dale I know.

Joe A grown man, isn't that something?

Scene 27

Collins and Skippy on the Bridge

Collins *has been in control of the boat.* **Skippy** *comes on the bridge.*

Skippy Yo, Mr Collins.

Collins Yessir.

Skippy We pick up the mail?

Collins Yes *sir*.

Skippy Good.

Collins We got that report on Guiliani.

Skippy That's fine. Get me something to eat.

Collins Yessir. (*Spotting* **Joe**.) Yo, Litko!

Joe Yo . . . !

Scene 28

In the Galley

Fred I don't give a fuck; the man lived on the sea, the man *died* on the sea.

Dale He died on land.

Fred He died 'cause *of* the sea. 'Cause of the sea. 'Cause of his *trade*. You understand?

Dale Yeah.

Fred Good.

Pause.

Dale He died 'cause of his desires.

Pause.

Fred Yeah.

Pause.

Well, we all *have* 'em . . .

Pause.

Dale You know him well?

Fred I knew him *very* well, Dale, *very* well.

Joe *enters the galley.*

Fred Yo, Joe . . . !

Joe Yo, Fred.

Fred I'm telling my man about Guiliani.

Joe Yeah. They called the ship. We're picking him up in Duluth.

Fred We're picking *who* up?

Joe What?

Fred *Who* we're picking up?

Joe Guigliani.

Fred We're picking up Guigliani?

Joe Yeah. He caught the train.

Fred He caught the train to Duluth?

Joe Yeah.

Pause.

Fred How come he missed the boat?

Joe Yeah. Skippy said he said his aunt died, but he thinks the *real* reason 'cause he overslept.

Fred . . . sonofabitch . . .

Joe Well. I'll be glad to have him back.

Fred *Oh* yeah . . .

Dale You want a cup of coffee?

Joe Thank you.

Collins, *on the bridge, is seen talking into the ship-to-shore radio.*

Collins W.A.Y. Chicago, this is the *T. Harrison* en route.
Pause.
I read you five-by-five.

Edmond

Hokey Pokey Wickey Wamm
Salacapinkus Muley Comm
Tamsey Wamsey Wierey Wamm
King of the Cannibal Islands

— Popular song

To Richard Nelson and Wally Shawn

The Characters:

Fortune-Teller
Edmond, *a man in his mid thirties*
His Wife
A Man in a Bar
A B-Girl
A Bartender
The Manager
A Peep Show Girl
Three Gamblers
A Card Sharp
A Bystander
Two Shills
A Leafleteer
A Manager, *female*
A Whore
A Hotel Clerk
A Pawnshop Owner
A Customer
The Man in Back
A Woman in the Subway
A Pimp
Glenna, *a waitress*
A Tramp
A Mission Preacher
A Policeman
An Interrogator
A Prisoner
A Chaplain
A Guard

Setting: New York City

The world première of *Edmond* was produced by the
Goodman Theater, Chicago, Illinois, on 4 June 1982, with
the following cast:

A Mission Preacher/A Prisoner	Paul Butler
The Manager/A Leafleteer/	
A Customer/A Policeman/A Guard	Rich Cluchey
A B-Girl/A Whore	Joyce Hazard
A Peep Show Girl/Glenna	Laura Innes
A Man in a Bar/A Hotel Clerk/	
The Man in Back/A Chaplain	Bruce Jarchow
Edmond's Wife	Linda Kimbrough
Fortune-Teller/A Manager/	
A Woman in the Subway	Marge Kotlisky
A Shill/A Pimp	Ernest Perry, Jr
A Cardsharp/A Guard	José Santana
Edmond	Colin Stinton
A Bartender/A Bystander/	
A Pawnshop Owner/	
An Interrogator	Jack Wallace

Directed by Gregory Mosher
Settings by Bill Bartelt
Lighting by Kevin Rigdon
Costumes by Marsha Kowal
Fight choreography by David Woolley
Stage managers Tom Biscotto, Anne Clarke

The New York production opened at the Provincetown
Playhouse on 27 October 1982, with Lionel Mark Smith
playing the roles of a **Shill/Pimp**.

The British première of *Edmond* was a joint production by the Tyne Wear Company, Newcastle-upon-Tyne, and the Royal Court Theatre, London. It opened at the Newcastle Playhouse on 7 November 1985, and at the Royal Court on 3 December 1985. The cast was as follows:

Edmond	Colin Stinton
Fortune-Teller/Peep Show Girl/Glenna	Miranda Richardson
Edmond's Wife	Connie Booth
Man in Bar/Hotel Clerk/Man in Back/Guard	Linal Haft
B-Girl/Whore/Woman in Subway	Marion McLoughlin
Bartender/Shill/Pimp	Cyril Nri
Manager/Cardsharp/Leafleteer/Customer/Interrogator	William Armstrong
Bystander/Pawnshop Owner/Policeman/Chaplain	Sam Douglas
Preacher/Prisoner	George Harris

Directed by Richard Eyre
Designed by William Dudley
Lighting by Mark Henderson
Sound Designer Dave Cross
Assistant Director Hettie Macdonald
Casting Director Serena Hill

Scenes

Scene 1

The Fortune-Teller

Edmond and the **Fortune-Teller** seated across the table from each other.

Fortune-Teller If things are predetermined surely they must manifest themselves.

When we look back – as we look back – we see that we could never have done otherwise than as we did. (*Pause.*)

Surely, then, there must have been signs.

If only we could have read them. We say, 'I see now that I could not have done otherwise . . . my *diet* caused me. Or my stars . . . which caused me to eat what I ate . . . or my *genes*, or some other thing beyond my control forced me to act as I did . . .'

And those things which *forced* us, of course, must make their signs: our *diet*, or our *genes*, or our *stars*.

Pause.

And there *are* signs. (*Pause.*)

What we see reflects (more than what is) what is to be.

Pause.

Are you cold?

Edmond No. (*Pause.*)

Fortune-Teller Would you like me to close the window?

Edmond No, thank you.

Fortune-Teller Give me your palm.

Edmond *does so.*

Fortune-Teller You are not where you belong. It is perhaps true none of us are, but in your case this is more true than in most.

We all like to believe we are special. In your case this is true.

Listen to me. (*She continues talking as the lights dim.*)
The world seems to be crumbling around us. You look and
you wonder if what you perceive is accurate. And you are
unsure what your place is. To what extent you are cause and
to what an effect . . .

Scene 2

At Home

Edmond *and his* **Wife** *are sitting in the living room. A pause.*

Wife The girl broke the lamp. (*Pause.*)

Edmond Which lamp?

Wife The antique lamp.

Edmond In my room?

Wife Yes. (*Pause.*)

Edmond Huh.

Wife That lamp cost over two hundred and twenty dollars.

Edmond (*pause*) Maybe we can get it fixed.

Wife We're never going to get it fixed.
I think that that's the *point* . . .
I think that's why she did it.

Edmond Yes. Alright – I'm going. (*Pause. He gets up and
starts out of the room.*)

Wife Will you bring me back some cigarettes . . .

Edmond I'm not coming back.

Wife What?

Edmond I'm not coming back. (*Pause.*)

Wife What do you mean?

Edmond I'm going, and I'm not going to come back.
(*Pause.*)

Wife You're not *ever* coming back?

Edmond No.

Wife Why not? (*Pause.*)

Edmond I don't want to live this kind of life.

Wife What does that mean?

Edmond That I can't live this life.

Wife 'You can't live this life' so you're leaving me.

Edmond Yes.

Wife Ah. Ah. Ah.
And what about ME?
Don't you *love* me anymore?

Edmond No.

Wife You don't.

Edmond No.

Wife And why is that?

Edmond I don't know.

Wife And when did you find this out?

Edmond A long time ago.

Wife You did.

Edmond Yes.

Wife How long ago?

Edmond Years ago.

Wife You've known for years that you don't love me.

Edmond Yes. (*Pause.*)

Wife Oh. (*Pause.*) Then why did you decide you're leaving *now?*

Edmond I've had enough.

Wife Yes. But why *now?*

Edmond (*pause*) Because you don't interest me spiritually or sexually. (*Pause.*)

Wife Hadn't you known this for some time?

Edmond What do you think?

Wife I think you did.

Edmond Yes, I did.

Wife And why didn't you leave *then?*
Why didn't you leave *then*, you stupid *shit!!!*
All of these years you say that you've been living here? . . .

Pause.

Eh? You idiot . . .
I've had enough.
You idiot . . . to see you passing *judgment* on me all this
time . . .

Edmond . . . I never judged you . . .

Wife . . . and then you tell me. 'You're leaving.'

Edmond Yes.

Wife *Go*, then . . .

Edmond I'll call you.

Wife Please. And we'll talk. What shall we do with the
house? Cut it in half?
Go. Get out of here. Go.

Edmond You think that I'm fooling.

Wife I do *not*. Goodbye. Thank you. Goodbye.
(*Pause.*) Goodbye. (*Pause.*)
Get *out*. Get *out* of here.
And don't you *ever* come back.
Do you hear me?

Wife *exits. Closing the door on him.*

Scene 3

A Bar

Edmond *is at the bar. A* **Man** *is next to him. They sit for a while.*

Man . . . I'll tell you who's got it *easy* . . .

Edmond Who?

Man The niggers. (*Pause.*) Sometimes I wish I was a nigger.

Edmond Sometimes I do, too.

Man I'd rob a store. I don't blame them.
I swear to God. Because I want to tell you: we're *bred* to do
the things that we do.

Edmond Mm.

Man Northern races *one* thing, and the southern races
something else. And what *they* want to do is sit beneath the
tree and watch the elephant. (*Pause.*) And I don't blame
them one small bit. Because there's too much *pressure* on us.

Edmond Yes.

Man And that's no joke, and that's not *poetry*, it's just too
much.

Edmond It is. It absolutely is.

Man A man's got to get *out* . . .

Edmond What do you mean?

Man A man's got to get *away* from himself . . .

Edmond . . . that's true . . .

Man . . . because the pressure is too much.

Edmond What do you do?

Man What do you mean?

Edmond What do you do to get out?

Man What do I do?

Edmond Yes.

Man What are the things to do? What are the things *anyone* does? . . . (*Pause.*)
Pussy . . . I don't know . . . *Pussy* . . . *Power* . . . *Money* . . . uh . . . *adventure* . . . (*Pause.*)
I think that's it . . . uh, self-*destruction* . . .
I think that that's it . . . don't you? . . .

Edmond Yes.

Man . . . uh, *religion* . . . I suppose that's it, uh, *release*, uh, ratification. (*Pause*)
You have to get *out*, you have to get something opens your *nose*, life is too short.

Edmond My wife and I are incompatible.

Man I'm sorry to hear that. (*Pause.*)
In what way?

Edmond I don't find her attractive.

Man Mm.

Edmond It's a boring thing to talk about. But that's what's on my mind.

Man I understand.

Edmond You do?

Man Yes. (*Pause.*)

Edmond Thank you.

Man Believe me, that's alright. I know that we all *need* it, and we don't know where to *get* it, and I know what it *means*, and I understand.

Edmond . . . I feel . . .

Man I know. Like your balls were cut off.

Edmond Yes. A long, long time ago.

Man Mm-hm.

Edmond And I don't feel like a man.

Man Do you know what you need?

Edmond No.

Man You need to get laid.

Edmond I do. I know I do.

Man That's why the niggers have it easy.

Edmond Why?

Man I'll tell you why: there are responsibilities they never have accepted. (*Pause.*)
Try the Allegro.

Edmond What is that?

Man A bar on Forty-seventh Street.

Edmond Thank you.

*The **Man** gets up, pays for drinks.*

Man I want this to be on me. I want you to *remember* there was someone who listened. (*Pause.*)
You'd do the same for me.

*The **Man** exits.*

Scene 4

The Allegro

Edmond *sits by himself for a minute. A* **B-Girl** *comes by.*

B-Girl You want to buy me a drink?

Edmond Yes. (*Pause.*)
I'm putting myself at your *mercy* . . . this is my first time in a place like this. I don't want to be taken advantage of.

Pause.

You understand?

B-Girl Buy me a drink and we'll go in the back.

Edmond And do what?

B-Girl Whatever you want.

Edmond *leans over and whispers to* **B-Girl**.

B-Girl Ten dollars.

Edmond Alright.

B-Girl Buy me a drink.

Edmond You get a commission on the drinks?

B-Girl Yes.

She gestures to **Bartender**, *who brings drinks.*

Edmond How much commission do you get?

B-Girl Fifty percent.

Bartender (*bringing drinks*) That's twenty bucks.

Edmond (*getting up*) It's too much.

Bartender What?

Edmond Too much. Thank you.

B-Girl Ten!

Edmond No, thank you.

B-Girl Ten!

Edmond I'll give you five. I'll give you the five you'd get for
the drink if I gave them ten.
But I'm not going to give them ten.

B-Girl But you have to buy me a drink.

Edmond I'm sorry. No.

B-Girl Alright. (*Pause.*) Give me ten.

Edmond On top of the ten?

B-Girl Yeah. You give me twenty.

Edmond I should give you twenty.

B-Girl Yes.

Edmond To *you*.

B-Girl Yes.

Edmond And then you give him the five?

B-Girl Yes. I got to give him the five.

Edmond No.

B-Girl For the *drink*.

Edmond No. You don't have to pay him for the drink. It's *tea* . . .

B-Girl It's not tea.

Edmond It's not tea!? . . .

He drinks.

If it's not *tea* what *is* it, then? . . .
I came here to be *straight* with you, why do we have to go *through* this? . . .

Manager Get in or get out. (*Pause.*)
Don't mill around.
Get in or get out . . . (*Pause.*)
Alright.

Manager *escorts* **Edmond** *out of the bar.*

Scene 5

A Peep Show

Booths with closed doors all around. A **Girl** *in a spangled leotard sees* **Edmond** *and motions him to a booth whose door she is opening.*

Girl Seven. Go in Seven. (*He starts to Booth Seven.*)
No. Six! I mean Six. Go in Six.

He goes into Booth Six. She disappears behind the row of booths, and appears behind a plexiglass partition in Booth Six.

Girl Take your dick out. (*Pause.*)
Take your dick out. (*Pause.*)
Come on. Take your dick out.

Edmond I'm not a cop.

Girl I know you're not a cop. Take your dick out.
I'm gonna give you a good time.

Edmond How can we get this barrier to come down?

Girl It doesn't come down.

Edmond Then how are you going to give me a good time?

Girl Come here.

He leans close. She whispers.

Give me ten bucks. (*Pause.*)
Give me ten bucks. (*Pause.*)
Put it through the thing.

She indicates a small ventilator hole in the plexiglass. Pause.

Put it through the thing.

Edmond (*checking his wallet*) I haven't got ten bucks.

Girl Okay . . . just . . . yes.
Okay. Give me the twenty.

Edmond Are you going to give me change?

Girl Yes. Just give me the twenty. Give it to me.
Good. Now take your dick out.

Edmond Can I have my ten?

Girl Look. Let me hold the ten.

Edmond Give me my ten back. (*Pause.*)
Come on. Give me my ten back.

Girl Let me hold the ten . . .

Edmond Give me my ten back and I'll give you a tip when you're done.

Pause. She does so.

Thank you.

Girl Okay. Take your dick out.

Edmond (*of the plexiglass*) How does this thing come down?

Girl It doesn't come down.

Edmond It doesn't come down?

Girl No.

Edmond Then what the fuck am I giving you ten bucks for?

Girl Look: You can touch me. Stick your finger in this you can touch me.

Edmond I don't want to touch *you* . . .
I want *you* to touch *me* . . .

Girl I can't. (*Pause.*) I would, but I can't. We'd have the cops in here. We would.
Honestly. (*Pause.*)
Look: Put your finger in here . . . come on.
(*Pause.*) Come on.

He zips his pants up and leaves the booth.

You're only cheating your*self* . . .

Scene 6

On the Street, Three-Card Monte

A **Cardsharp**, *a* **Bystander** *and two* **Shills**.

Sharper You pick the red you win, and twenty get you forty. Put your money up.
The *black* gets *back*, the *red* you go ahead . . .
Who saw the red? . . . Who saw the red?
Who saw her? . . .

Bystander (*to* **Edmond**) The fellow over there is a shill . . .

Edmond Who is? . . .

Bystander (*points*) You want to know how to beat the game?

Edmond How?

Bystander You figure out which card has *got* to win . . .

Edmond Uh-huh . . .

Bystander . . . and bet the *other* one.

Sharper Who saw the red? . . .

Bystander They're all shills, they're all part of an act.

Sharper Who saw her? Five will get you ten . . .

Shill (*playing lookout*) Cops . . . cops . . . cops . . . *don't run* . . . *don't run* . . .

Everyone scatters. **Edmond** *moves down the street.*

Scene 7

Passing Out Leaflets

Edmond *moves down the street. A* **Man** *is passing out leaflets.*

Leafleteer Check it out . . . check it out . . .
This is what you looking for . . . Take it . . .
I'm *giving* you something . . . *Take* it . . .

Edmond *takes the leaflet.*

Now: Is that what you looking for or not? . . .

Edmond (*reading the leaflet*) Is this true? . . .

Leafleteer Would I give it to you if it wasn't? . . .

Edmond *walks off reading the leaflet. The* **Leafleteer** *continues with his spiel.*

Check it out . . .

Scene 8

The Whorehouse

Edmond *shows up with the leaflet. He talks to the* **Manager**, *a woman.*

Manager Hello.

Edmond Hello.

Manager Have you been here before?

Edmond No.

Manager How'd you hear about us? (**Edmond** *shows her the leaflet.*) You from out of town?

Edmond Yes. What's the deal here?

Manager This is a *health* club.

Edmond . . . I know.

Manager And our rates are by the hour. (*Pause.*)

Edmond Yes?

Manager Sixty-eight dollars for the first hour, sauna, free bar, showers . . . (*Pause.*)
The hour doesn't start until you and the masseuse are in the room.

Edmond Alright.

Manager Whatever happens in the room, of course, is between you.

Edmond I understand.

Manager You understand?

Edmond Yes.

Manager . . . Or, for two hours it's one hundred fifty dollars. If you want two hostesses that is two hundred dollars for one hour. (*Pause.*) Whatever arrangement that you choose to make with *them* is between *you.*

Edmond Good. (*Pause.*)

Manager What would you like?

Edmond One hour.

Manager You pay that now. How would you like to pay?

Edmond How can I pay?

Manager With cash or credit card. The billing for the card will read 'Atlantic Ski and Tennis'.

Edmond I'll pay you with cash.

Scene 9

Upstairs at the Whorehouse

Edmond *and the* **Whore** *are in a cubicle.*

Whore How are you?

Edmond Fine. I've never done this before.

Whore No? (*She starts rubbing his neck.*)

Edmond No. That feels very good. (*Pause.*)

Whore You've got a good body.

Edmond Thank you.

Whore Do you work out? (*Pause.*)

Edmond I jog.

Whore Mmm. (*Pause.*)

Edmond And I used to play football in high school.

Whore You've kept yourself in good shape.

Edmond Thank you.

Whore (*pause*) What shall we do?

Edmond I'd like to have intercourse with you.

Whore That sounds very nice. I'd like that, too.

Edmond You would?

Whore Yes.

Edmond How much would that be?

Whore For a straight fuck, that would be a hundred fifty.

Edmond That's too much.

Whore You know that I'm giving you a break . . .

Edmond . . . no . . .

Whore . . . Because this is your first time here . . .

Edmond No. It's too much, on top of the sixty-eight at the door . . .

Whore I know, I know, but you know, I don't get to keep it all. I *split* it with them. Yes. They don't pay me, I pay *them*.

Edmond It's too much. (*Pause. The* **Whore** *sighs.*)

Whore How much do you have?

Edmond All I had was one hundred for the whole thing.

Whore You mean a hundred for it all.

Edmond That only left me thirty.

Whore Noooo, honey, you couldn't get a *thing* for that.

Edmond Well, how much do you want?

Whore (*sighs*) Alright, for a straight fuck, one hundred twenty.

Edmond I couldn't pay that.

Whore I'm sorry, then. It would have been nice.

Edmond I'll give you eighty.

Whore No.

Edmond One hundred.

Whore Alright, but only, you know, 'cause this is your first time.

Edmond I know.

Whore . . . 'cause we *split* with them, you understand . . .

Edmond I understand.

Whore Alright. One hundred.

Edmond Thank you. I appreciate this. (*Pause.*)
Would it offend you if I wore a rubber? . . .

Whore Not at all. (*Pause.*)

Edmond Do you have one? . . .

Whore Yes. (*Pause.*) You want to pay me now? . . .

Edmond Yes. Certainly. (*He takes out his wallet, hands her a credit card.*)

Whore I need cash, honey.

Edmond They said at the door I could pay with my . . .

Whore . . . That was at the door . . .
you have to pay *me* with *cash* . . .

Edmond I don't think I *have* it . . . (*He checks through his wallet.*) I don't *have* it . . .

Whore How much do you have? . . .

Edmond I, uh, only have *sixty*.

Whore Jeez, I'm *sorry*, honey, but I can't *do* it . . .

Edmond Well, wait, wait, wait, wait, maybe we could . . . wait . . .

Whore Why don't you *get* it, and come *back* here . . .

Edmond Well, where could I *get* it? . . .

Whore Go to a restaurant and cash a check, I'll be here till *four* . . .

Edmond I'll. I'll . . . um, um . . . *yes. Thank* you . . .

Whore Not at all.

Edmond *leaves the whorehouse.*

Scene 10

Three-Card Monte

Edmond *out on the street, passes by the three-card-monte men, who have assembled again.*

Sharper You can't win if you don't play . . . (*To* **Edmond***.*) *You*, sir . . .

Edmond Me? . . .

Sharper You going to try me again? . . .

Edmond Again? . . .

Sharper *I* remember you beat me out of that *fifty* that time
with your girlfriend . . .

Edmond . . . When was this?

Sharper On four*teen*ff street . . .
You going to try me one more time? . . .

Edmond Uh . . .

Sharper . . . Play you for that fifty . . . Fifty get you one
hundred, we see you as fast as you was . . .
Pay on the red, pass on the black . . .
Where is the queen? . . . You pick the queen you win . . .
Where is the queen? . . . Who saw the queen? . . .
You put up fifty, win a hundred . . . Now: Who saw the
queen? . . .

Shill I got her!

Sharper How much? Put your money up. How much?

Shill I bet you fifty dollars.

Sharper Put it up.

The **Shill** *does so. The* **Shill** *turns a card.*

Shill There!

Sharper My man, I'm jus' too quick for you today.
Who saw the queen? We got two cards left.
Pay on the *red* queen, who saw her?

Edmond I saw her.

Sharper Ah, *shit*, man, you too fass for me.

Edmond . . . For fifty dollars . . .

Sharper Alright – alright.
Put it up. (*Pause.*)

Edmond Will you pay me if I win?

Sharper Yes, I will. If you win. But you got to *win* first . . .

Edmond All that I've got to do is turn the queen.

Sharper Thass all you got to do.

Edmond I'll bet you fifty.

Sharper You sure?

Edmond Yes. I'm sure.

Sharper Put it up. (**Edmond** *does so*.) Now: Which one you like?

Edmond (*turning card*) There!

Sharper (*taking money*) I'm *sorry*, my man. This time you lose –

now we even. Take another shot. You pick the queen you win . . . bet you another fifty . . .

Edmond Let me see those cards.

Sharper These cards are fine, it's you thass slow.

Edmond I want to see the cards.

Sharper These cards are good my man, you *lost*.

Edmond You let me see those cards.

Sharper You ain't goin' *see* no motherfuckin' cards, man, we playin' a *game* here . . .

Shill . . . You lost, *get* lost.

Edmond Give me those cards, fella.

Sharper You want to see the cards? You want to see the cards? . . . *Here* is the motherfuckin' cards . . .

He hits **Edmond** *in the face. He and the* **Shill** *beat* **Edmond** *for several seconds.* **Edmond** *falls to the ground.*

Scene 11

A Hotel

Edmond, *torn and battered, comes up to the* **Desk Clerk**.

Edmond I want a room.

Clerk Twenty-two dollars. (*Pause.*)

Edmond I lost my wallet.

Clerk Go to the police.

Edmond You can call up American Express.

Clerk Go to the police. (*Pause.*)
I don't want to hear it.

Edmond You can call the credit-card people. I have insurance.

Clerk Call them yourself. Right across the hall.

Edmond I have no money.

Clerk I'm sure it's a free call.

Edmond Do those phones require a dime?

Clerk (*pause*) I'm sure I don't know.

Edmond You know if they need a *dime* or not.
To get a *dial* tone . . . You know if they need a *dime*, for chrissake. Do you want to live in this kind of world?
Do you want to live in a *world* like that? I've been *hurt?*
Are you *blind?* Would you appreciate it if I acted this way to *you?* (*Pause.*)
I *asked* you one simple thing.
Do they need a *dime?*

Clerk No. They don't need a dime. Now, you make your call, and you go somewhere else.

Scene 12

The Pawnshop

*The **Owner** waiting on a customer who is perusing objects in the display counter.*

Customer Whaddaya get for that? What is that?
Fourteen or eighteen karat?

Owner Fourteen.

Customer Yeah? Lemme see that. How much is that?

Owner Six hundred eighty-five.

Customer Why is that? How old is that? Is that *old?*

Owner You know how much *gold* that you got in there? Feel. That. Just feel that.

Customer Where is it marked?

Owner Right there. You want that loupe?

Customer No. I can see it.

Edmond *comes into the store and stands by the two.*

Owner (*to* **Edmond**) What?

Edmond I want to pawn something.

Owner Talk to the man in back.

Customer What else you got like this?

Owner I don't know *what* I got. You're *looking* at it.

Customer (*pointing to item in display case*) Lemme see that.

Edmond (*goes to* **Man** *in back behind grate*) I want to pawn something.

Man What?

Edmond My ring. (*Holds up hand.*)

Man Take it off.

Edmond It's difficult to take it off.

Man Spit on it. (**Edmond** *does so.*)

Customer How much is that?

Owner Two hundred twenty.

Edmond (*happily*) I got it off. (*He hands the ring to the* **Man**.)

Man What do you want to do with this?
You want to pawn it.

Edmond Yes. How does that work?

Man Is that what you want to do?

Edmond Yes. Are there other things to do?

Man . . . What you can *do*, no, I mean, if you wanted it *appraised* . . .

Edmond . . . Uh-huh . . .

Man . . . or want to *sell* it . . .

Edmond . . . Uh-huh . . .

Man . . . or you wanted it to *pawn* . . .

Edmond I understand.

Man Alright?

Edmond How much is getting it appraised?

Man Five dollars.

Customer Lemme see something in black.

Edmond What would you give me if I pawned it?

Man What do you want for it?

Edmond What is it worth?

Man You pawn it all you're gonna get's approximately . . . You know how this works?

Customer Yes. Let me see that . . .

Edmond No.

Man What you get, a quarter of the value.

Edmond Mm.

Man Approximately. For a year. You're paying twelve percent. You can redeem your pledge with the year you pay your twelve percent. To that time. Plus the amount of the loan.

Edmond What is my pledge?

Man Well, that depends on what it *is*.

Edmond What do you mean?

Man What it *is*. Do you understand?

Edmond No.

Man Whatever the amount *is*, that is your pledge.

Edmond The amount of the loan.

Man That's right.

Edmond I understand.

Man Alright. What are you looking for, the ring?

Customer Nope. Not today. I'll catch you next time. Lemme see that knife.

Edmond What is it worth?

Man The most I can give you, hundred and twenty bucks.

Customer This is nice.

Edmond I'll take it.

Man Good. I'll be right back. Give me the ring.

Edmond *does so.* **Edmond** *wanders over to watch the other transaction.*

Customer (*holding up knife*) What are you asking for this?

Owner Twenty-three bucks. Say, twenty bucks.

Customer (*to himself*) Twenty bucks . . .

Edmond Why is it so expensive?

Owner Why is it so expensive?

Customer No. I'm going to pass. (*He hands knife back, exiting.*) I'll catch you later.

Owner Right.

Edmond Why is the knife so expensive?

Owner This is a *survival* knife. GI Issue. World War Two. And that is why.

Edmond Survival knife.

Owner That is correct.

Edmond Is it a good knife?

Owner It is the best knife that money can buy.

He starts to put knife away. As an afterthought:

You want it?

Edmond Let me think about it for a moment.

Scene 13

The Subway

Edmond *is in the subway. Waiting with him is a* **Woman** *in a hat.*

Edmond (*pause*) My mother had a hat like that. (*Pause.*)
My mother had a hat like that. (*Pause.*) I . . . I'm not making
conversation. She wore it for years. She had it when I was a
child.

The **Woman** *starts to walk away.* **Edmond** *grabs her.*

Edmond I wasn't just making it *up*. It *happened* . . .

Woman (*detaching herself from his grip*) Excuse me . . .

Edmond . . . who the fuck do you think you *are?* . . .
I'm *talking* to you . . . What am I? A *stone?* . . .
Did I say, 'I want to lick your pussy'? . . .
I said, 'My mother had that same hat . . .'
You *cunt* . . . What am I? A *dog?* I'd like to slash your fucking
face . . . I'd like to slash your motherfucking *face* apart . . .

Woman . . . WILL SOMEBODY *HELP ME* . . .

Edmond *You* don't know who I am . . . (*She breaks free.*) Is
everybody in this town *insane?* . . . Fuck you . . . fuck you . . .
fuck you . . . fuck the *lot* of you . . . fuck you *all* . . . I don't
need you . . . I worked all of my life!

Scene 14

On the Street, outside the Peep Show

Pimp What are you looking for?

Edmond What?

Pimp What are you looking for?

Edmond I'm not looking for a goddamn thing.

Pimp You looking for that *joint*, it's *closed*.

Edmond What joint?

Pimp That *joint* that you was looking for.

Edmond Thank you, no. I'm not looking for that joint.

Pimp You looking for *something*, and I think that I know what you looking for.

Edmond You do?

Pimp You come with me, I get you what you want.

Edmond What do I want?

Pimp *I* know. We get you some *action*, my friend.
We get you something sweet to shoot on. (*Pause.*)
I know. Thass what I'm doing here.

Edmond What are you saying?

Pimp I'm saying that we going to find you something nice.

Edmond You're saying that you're going to find me a woman.

Pimp Thass what I'm *doing* out here, friend.

Edmond How much?

Pimp Well, how much do you want?

Edmond I want somebody clean.

Pimp Thass right.

Edmond I want a blow-job.

Pimp Alright.

Edmond How much?

Pimp Thirty bucks.

Edmond That's too much.

Pimp How much do you want to *spen'*? . . .

Edmond Say fifteen dollars.

Pimp Twenny-five.

Edmond No. Twenty.

Pimp Yes.

Edmond Is that alright?

Pimp Give me the twenty.

Edmond I'll give it to you when we see the girl.

Pimp Hey, I'm not going to *leave* you, man, you *coming* with me. We *goin'* to see the girl.

Edmond Good. I'll give it to you then.

Pimp You give it to me *now*, you unnerstan'? Huh? (*Pause.*) Thass the trans*action*. (*Pause.*) You see? Unless you were a *cop*. (*Pause.*) You give me the *money*, and then thass entra*p*ment. (*Pause.*) You understand?

Edmond Yes. I'm not a cop.

Pimp Alright.
Do you *see* what I'm saying?

Edmond I'm sorry.

Pimp Thass alright. (**Edmond** *takes out wallet. Exchange of money*.) You come with me. Now we'll just walk here like we're talking.

Edmond Is she going to be clean?

Pimp Yes, she is. I understand you, man.

Pause. They walk.

I understand what you want. (*Pause.*) Believe me.

Pause.

Edmond Is there any money in this?

Pimp Well, you know, man, there's *some* . . . you get done piecing off the *police*, this man *here* . . . the *medical*, the *bills*, *you* know.

Edmond How much does the girl get?

Pimp Sixty percent.

Edmond Mm.

Pimp *Oh* yeah. (*He indicates a spot.*) Up here.

They walk to the spot. The **Pimp** *takes out a knife and holds it to* **Edmond**'s *neck.*

Pimp Now give me all you' money mothafucka! *Now!*

Edmond Alright.

Pimp *All* of it. Don't turn aroun' . . . don't turn aroun' . . . just put it in my hand.

Edmond Alright.

Pimp . . . And don't you make a motherfuckin' sound . . .

Edmond I'm going to do everything that you say . . .

Pimp Now you just han' me all you got.

Edmond *turns, strikes the* **Pimp** *in the face.*

Edmond YOU MOTHERFUCKING NIGGER!

Pimp Hold on . . .

Edmond You motherfucking *shit* . . . you *jungle* bunny . . . (*He strikes the* **Pimp** *again. He drops his knife.*)

Pimp I . . .

Edmond You *coon*, you *cunt*, you *cock*sucker . . .

Pimp I . . .

Edmond 'Take me upstairs'? . . .

Pimp Oh, my God . . . (*The* **Pimp** *has fallen to the sidewalk and* **Edmond** *is kicking him.*)

Edmond You *fuck*. You *nigger*. You dumb *cunt* . . .
You *shit* . . . You shit . . . (*Pause.*)
You fucking *nigger*. (*Pause.*) Don't fuck with *me*, you *coon* . . .

Pause. **Edmond** *spits on him.*

I hope you're *dead*.

Pause.

Don't fuck with *me*, you *coon* . . .

Pause. **Edmond** *spits on him.*

Scene 15

The Coffeehouse

Edmond *seated in the coffeehouse, addresses the waitress,* **Glenna**.

Edmond I want a cup of coffee. No. A beer.
Beer chaser. Irish whiskey.

Glenna Irish whiskey.

Edmond Yes. A double. Huh.

Glenna You're in a peppy mood today.

Edmond You're goddamn right I am, and you want me to tell you *why?* Because I am *alive*. You know how much of our life we're alive, you and me? *Nothing*. Two minutes out of the year. You know, you know, we're *sheltered* . . .

Glenna Who is?

Edmond You and I. White people. All of us. All of us. We're doomed. The white race is doomed. And do you know *why?* . . . Sit down . . .

Glenna I can't. I'm working.

Edmond And do you know *why* – you can do anything you *want* to do, you don't sit down because you're '*working*', the

reason you don't sit down is you don't *want* to sit down,
because it's more comfortable to *accept* a law than question it
and live your life. All of us. *All* of us.
We've bred the life out of ourselves. And we live in a fog.
We live in a dream. Our life is a *school*house, and we're dead.

Pause.

How old are you?

Glenna   Twenty-eight.

Edmond   I've lived in a fog for thirty-four years.
Most of the life I have to live. It's gone.
It's gone. I wasted it. Because I didn't know. And you know
what the answer is? To *live*. (*Pause*.)
I want to go home with you tonight.

Glenna   Why?

Edmond   Why do you think? I want to fuck you.
(*Pause*.) It's as simple as that.
What's your name?

Glenna   Glenna. (*Pause*.) What's yours?

Edmond   Edmond.

Scene 16

Glenna's Apartment

Edmond *and* **Glenna** *are lounging around semiclothed.* **Edmond**
shows **Glenna** *the survival knife.*

Edmond   You see this?

Glenna   Yes.

Edmond   That fucking nigger comes up to me, what am I
fitted to do. He comes up, 'Give me all your money.' Thirty-
four years fits me to sweat and say he's underpaid, and he
can't get a *job*, he's *bigger* than me . . . he's a *killer*, he don't
care about his *life*, you understand, so he'd do *anything* . . .

Eh? That's what I'm fitted to do. In a mess of intellectuality
to wet my *pants* while this *coon* cuts my *dick* off . . . eh? Because
I'm taught to *hate*.
I want to tell you something. Something *spoke* to me, I got a
shock (I don't know, I got mad . . .), I got a *shock*, and I spoke
back to him. 'Up your *ass*, you *coon* . . . you want to fight, *I'll*
fight you, I'll cut out your fuckin' *heart*, eh, *I* don't give a
fuck . . .'

Glenna Yes.

Edmond Eh? I'm saying, '*I* don't give a fuck, *I* got some
warlike blood in *my* veins, too, you fucking *spade*, you
coon . . .' The *blood* ran down his neck . . .

Glenna (*looking at knife*) With *that?*

Edmond You bet your ass . . .

Glenna Did you kill him?

Edmond Did I kill him?

Glenna Yes.

Edmond I don't care. (*Pause.*)

Glenna That's wonderful.

Edmond And in that *moment* . . .
when I *spoke*, you understand, 'cause that was more
important than the *knife*, when I spoke *back* to him, I
DIDN'T FUCKING WANT TO *UNDERSTAND* . . . let
him understand *me* . . .
I wanted to KILL him. (*Pause.*) In that *moment* thirty years of
prejudice came out of me. (*Pause.*) Thirty *years*. Of all those
um um um of all those *cleaning* ladies . . .

Glenna . . . Uh-huh . . .

Edmond . . . uh? . . . who *might* have broke the lamp.
SO WHAT? You understand? For the first *time*, I swear to God,
for the first *time* I saw: THEY'RE PEOPLE, TOO.

Glenna (*pause*) Do you know who I hate?

Edmond Who is that?

Glenna Faggots.

Edmond Yes. I hate them, too. And you know *why?*

Glenna Why?

Edmond They suck cock. (*Pause.*) And that's the truest thing you'll ever hear.

Glenna I hate them 'cause they don't like women.

Edmond They *hate* women.

Glenna I know that they do.

Edmond It makes you feel good to *say* it? Doesn't it?

Glenna Yes.

Edmond Then *say* it. Say it. If it makes you whole. *Always* say it. *Always* for your*self* . . .

Glenna It's hard.

Edmond *Yes*.

Glenna Sometimes it's hard.

Edmond You're goddamn right it's hard. And there's a *reason* why it's hard.

Glenna Why?

Edmond So that we will stand up. So that we'll be our *selves*. Glenna: (*Pause.*) Glenna: This world is a piece of shit. (*Pause.*) It is a shit house. (*Pause.*) . . . There is NO LAW . . . there is no *history* . . . there is just *now* . . . and if there is a *god* he may love the weak, Glenna. (*Pause.*) But he respects the strong. (*Pause.*) And if you are a *man* you should be feared. (*Pause.*) You should be *feared* . . . (*Pause.*)
You just know you command respect.

Glenna That's why I love the theater . . . (*Pause.*) *Because what you must ask respect for is yourself* . . .

Edmond What do you mean?

Glenna When you're on stage.

Edmond Yes.

Glenna For *your* feelings.

Edmond Absolutely. Absolutely, yes . . .

Glenna And, and, and *not* be someone else.

Edmond Why should you? . . .

Glenna . . . That's why, and I'm so proud to *be* in this profession . . .

Edmond . . . I don't blame you . . .

Glenna . . . because your aspirations . . .

Edmond . . . and I'll bet that you're good at it . . .

Glenna . . . they . . .

Edmond . . . They have no bounds.

Glenna There's nothing . . .

Edmond . . . Yes. I understand . . .

Glenna . . . to *bound* you but your soul.

Edmond (*pause*) Do something for me.

Glenna . . . Uh . . .

Edmond *Act* something for me. Would you act something for me? . . .

Glenna *Now?*

Edmond Yes.

Glenna Sitting right here? . . .

Edmond Yes. (*Pause.*)

Glenna Would you really like me to?

Edmond You know I would. You see me sitting here, and you know that I would. I'd *love* it.
Just because we both *want* to. I'd *love* you to. (*Pause.*)

Glenna What would you like me to do?

Edmond Whatever you'd like. What plays have you done?

Glenna Well, we've only done scenes.

Edmond You've only done scenes.

Glenna I shouldn't say 'only'. They contain the kernel of the play.

Edmond Uh-huh.

Pause.

What *plays* have you done?

Glenna In college I played Juliet.

Edmond In Shakespeare?

Glenna Yes. In Shakespeare. What do you think?

Edmond Well, I meant, there's *plays* named Juliet.

Glenna There are?

Edmond Yes.

Glenna I don't think so.

Edmond Well, there are. – Don't. Don't. Don't. Don't be so *limited* . . . And don't assume I'm dumb because I wear a suit and tie.

Glenna I don't assume that.

Edmond Because what we've *done* tonight. Since you met me, it didn't make a difference then. Forget it. All I meant, you say you are an *actress* . . .

Glenna I am an actress . . .

Edmond Yes. I say that's what you *say*. So *I* say what *plays* have you done. That's all.

Glenna The work I've done I have done for my peers.

Edmond What does that mean?

Glenna In class.

Edmond In class.

Glenna In class or workshop.

Edmond Not, not for a paying group.

Glenna No, absolutely not.

Edmond Then you are not an actress. Face it.
Let's start right. The two of us. I'm not lying to *you*, don't lie to *me*.
And don't lie to yourself.
Face it. You're a beautiful woman. You have *worlds* before you. I do, too.
Things to do. Things you can dis*cover*.
What I'm saying, start *now*, start *tonight*. With *me*. *Be* with me. Be what you *are* . . .

Glenna I am what I am.

Edmond That's absolutely right. And that's what I loved when I saw you tonight. What I *loved*.
I use that word. (*Pause*.) I used that word.
I loved a *woman*. Standing there. A working woman.
Who brought life to what she did. Who took a moment to *joke* with me. That's . . . that's . . . that's . . . God *bless* you what you are. Say it: I am a waitress.

Pause.

Say it.

Glenna What does it mean if I say something?

Edmond Say it with me. (*Pause*.)

Glenna What?

Edmond 'I am a waitress.'

Glenna I think that you better go.

Edmond If you want me to go I'll go.
Say it with me. Say what you are. And I'll say what *I* am.

Glenna . . . What *you* are . . .

Edmond I've *made* the discovery. Now: I want you to change your life with me. *Right* now, for what*ever* that we can be. *I* don't know what that is, *you* don't know. Speak with me. Right now. Say it.

Glenna I don't know what you're talking about.

Edmond Oh, by the Lord, yes, you do. Say it with me. (*She takes out a vial of pills*.) What are those?

Glenna Pills.

Edmond For what? Don't take them.

Glenna I have this tendency to get anxious.

Edmond (*knocks them from her hand*) Don't take them. Go *through* it. Go *through* with me.

Glenna You're scaring me.

Edmond I am not. I know when I'm scaring you. *Be*lieve me. (*Pause*.)

Glenna Get out. (*Pause*.)

Edmond Glenna. (*Pause*.)

Glenna Get out! GET OUT GET OUT! LEAVE ME THE FUCK ALONE!!! WHAT DID I DO, PLEDGE MY LIFE TO YOU? I LET YOU FUCK ME. GO AWAY.

Edmond Listen to me: You know what madness is?

Glenna I told you go away. (*Goes to phone. Dials*.)

Edmond I'm lonely, too. I know what it is, too. Believe me. Do you know what madness is?

Glenna (*into phone*) Susie? . . .

Edmond It's self-indulgence.

Glenna Suse, can you come over here? . . .

Edmond Will you please put that *down*? You know how *rare* this is? . . .

He knocks the phone out of her hands. **Glenna** *cowers.*

Glenna Oh fuck . . .

Edmond Don't be ridiculous. I'm *talking* to you.

Glenna Don't hurt me. No. No. I can't deal with this.

Edmond Don't be ridic . . .

Glenna I . . . No. Help! Help.

Edmond . . . You're being . . .

Glenna . . . HELP!

Edmond . . . are you *insane?* What the fuck are you trying to *do*, for godsake?

Glenna HELP!

Edmond You want to wake the *neighbors?*

Glenna WILL SOMEBODY HELP ME? . . .

Edmond Shut up shut up!

Glenna Will somebody help you are the get *away* from me! You are the *devil*. I know who you are. I know what you want me to do. Get *away* from me I curse *you*, you can't kill me, get away from me I'm *good*.

Edmond WILL YOU SHUT THE FUCK UP? You fucking *bitch*.
You're *nuts* . . .

He stabs her with the knife.

Are you *insane?* Are you *insane*, you fucking *idiot?* . . .
You stupid fucking *bitch* . . .
You stupid fucking . . . *now* look what you've done.

Pause.

Now look what you've bloody fucking done.

Scene 17

The Mission

Edmond *is attracted by the speech of a* **Mission Preacher**. *He walks to the front of the mission and listens outside the mission doors.*

Preacher 'Oh no, not me!' You say, 'Oh no, not me. Not *me*, Lord, to whom you hold out your hand. Not *me* to whom you offer your eternal grace. Not *me* who can be saved . . .'
But *who* but you, I ask you? *Who* but you.
You say you are a grievous sinner? He *knows* that you are.

You say he does not know the *depth* of my iniquity. *Believe* me,
friends, he does. And still you say, he does not know — you say
this in your secret soul — he does not know the terrible depth
of my unbelief.

Believe me friends, he knows that too.

To *all* of you who say his grace is not meant to extend to one
as black as you I say to WHO but you? To you *alone*. Not to
the blessed. You think that Christ died for the blessed? That
he died for the heavenly hosts? That did not make him God,
my friends, it does not need a God to sacrifice for angels. It
required a God to sacrifice for MAN. You hear me? For *you*
. . . there is *none* so black but that he died for you. He died
especially for you. Upon my life. On the graves of my family,
and by the surety I have of his Eternal Bliss HE DIED FOR
YOU AND YOU ARE SAVED. Praise *God*, my friends.
Praise God and testify. Who will come up and testify with
me, my friends? (*Pause.*)

Woman *from subway walks by. She sees* **Edmond** *and stares at
him.*

Edmond (*speaks up*) I will testify.

Preacher *Who* is that?

Edmond I will testify.

Preacher Sweet *God*, let that man come up here!

Edmond *starts into the church.*

Woman (*shouts*) That's the man! Someone! Call a
policeman! That's the man!

Preacher . . . Who will come open up his soul? Alleluia, my
friends. *Be* with me.

Woman That's the man. *Stop* him!

Edmond *stops and turns. He looks wonderingly at the* **Woman**,
then starts inside.

Policeman Just a moment, sir.

Edmond I . . . I . . . I . . . I . . . I'm on my way to church.

Preacher Sweet *Jesus*, let that man come forth . . .

Woman That's the man tried to rape me on the train. He had a knife . . .

Edmond . . . There must be some mistake . . .

Woman He tried to rape me on the train.

Edmond . . . There's some mistake, I'm on my way to church . . .

Policeman What's the trouble here?

Edmond No trouble, I'm on my way into the mission.

Woman This man tried to rape me on the train yesterday.

Edmond Obviously this woman's mad.

Preacher Will no one come forth?

Edmond I . . . I . . . I . . . have to go into the church.

Policeman Could I see some identification please?

Edmond Please, officer, I haven't time. I . . . I . . . it's been a long . . . I don't have my *wallet* on me. My name's Gregory Brock. I live at 428 Twenty-second Street, I own the building. I . . . I have to go inside the church.

Policeman You want to show me some ID?

Edmond I don't have any. I told you.

Policeman You're going to have to come with me.

Edmond I . . . please . . . Yes. In one minute.
Not . . . not now, I have to *preach* . . .

Policeman Come on.

Edmond You're, you're, you're making a . . .
Please. Let me go. And I'll come with you afterward.
I swear that I will. I swear it on my life.
There's been a mistake. I'm an elder in this church.
Come *with* me if you will.
I have to go and speak.

Policeman Look. (*Conciliatorily, he puts an arm on* **Edmond**. *He feels something. He pulls back*.) What's that?

Edmond It's nothing. (*The* **Policeman** *pulls out the survival knife*.) It's a knife. It's there for self-protection.

The **Policeman** *throws* **Edmond** *to the ground and handcuffs him*.

Scene 18

The Interrogation

Edmond *and an* **Interrogator** *at the police station*.

Interrogator What was the knife for?

Edmond For protection.

Interrogator From whom?

Edmond Everyone.

Interrogator You know that it's illegal?

Edmond No.

Interrogator It is.

Edmond (*pause*) I'm sorry.

Interrogator Speaking to that woman in the way you did is construed as assault.

Edmond I never spoke to her.

Interrogator She identified you as the man who accosted her last evening on the subway.

Edmond She is seriously mistaken.

Interrogator If she presses charges you'll be arraigned for assault.

Edmond For *speaking* to her?

Interrogator You admit that you were speaking to her?

Edmond (*pause*) I want to ask you something. (*Pause*.)

Interrogator Alright.

Edmond Did you ever kick a dog?

Pause.

Well, that's what I did. Man to man. That's what I did. I made a simple, harmless comment to her, she responded like a fucking bitch.

Interrogator You trying to pick her up?

Edmond Why should I try to pick her up?

Interrogator She was an attractive woman.

Edmond She was *not* an attractive woman.

Interrogator You gay?

Edmond What business is that of yours?

Interrogator Are you?

Edmond No.

Interrogator You married?

Edmond Yes. In fact. I was going back to my wife.

Interrogator You were going back to your wife?

Edmond I was going home to her.

Interrogator You said you were going back to her, what did you mean?

Edmond I'd left my wife, alright?

Interrogator You left your wife.

Edmond Yes.

Interrogator Why?

Edmond I was *bored*. Didn't that ever happen to *you*?

Interrogator And why did you lie to the officer?

Edmond What officer?

Interrogator Who picked you up. There's no Gregory
Brock at the address you gave. You didn't give him your
right name.

Edmond I was embarrassed.

Interrogator Why?

Edmond I didn't have my wallet.

Interrogator Why?

Edmond I'd left it at home.

Interrogator And why did that embarrass you?

Edmond I don't know. I have had no *sleep*. I just want to go
home. I am a *solid* . . . look: My name is Edmond Burke, I live
at 485 West Seventy-ninth Street. I work at Stearns and
Harrington. I had a tiff with my wife. I went out on the town.
I've learned my lesson. *Believe* me. I just want to go home.
Whatever I've done I'll make right. (*Pause.*) Alright?
(*Pause.*) Alright? These things happen and then they're done.
When he *stopped* me I was going to church. I've been unwell.
I'll confess to you that I've been confused, but, but . . . I've
learned my lesson and I'm ready to go home.

Interrogator Why did you kill that girl?

Edmond What girl?

Interrogator That girl you killed.

Scene 19

Jail

Edmond's wife *is visiting him. They sit across from each other in
silence for a while.*

Edmond How's everything?

Wife Fine. (*Pause.*)

Edmond I'm alright, too.

Wife Good. (*Pause.*)

Edmond You want to tell me you're *mad* at me or something?

Wife Did you kill that girl in her apartment?

Edmond Yes, but I want to tell you something . . . I didn't mean to. But do you want to hear something *funny?* . . .
(Now, don't laugh . . .) I think I'd just had too much coffee. (*Pause.*)
I'll tell you something else: I think there are just too many people in the world. I think that's why we kill each other. (*Pause.*) I . . . I . . . I suppose you're mad at me for leaving you. (*Pause.*) I don't suppose you're, uh, inclined (or, nor do I think you should be) to stand by me. I understand that. (*Pause.*) I'm sure that there are marriages where the wife would. Or the husband if it would go that way. (*Pause.*) But I know ours is not one of that type.
(*Pause.*) I know that you *wished* at one point it would be. I wished that too.
At one point. (*Pause.*)
I know at certain times we wished we could be . . . closer to each other. I can say that now. I'm sure this is the way you feel when someone near you dies. You never said the things you wanted desperately to say. It would have been so simple to say them. (*Pause.*) But you never did.

Wife You got the papers?

Edmond Yes.

Wife Good.

Edmond Oh, yes. I got them.

Wife Anything you need?

Edmond No. Can't think of a thing.

The **Wife** *stands up, starts gathering her things together.*

Edmond You take care, now!

Scene 20

The New Cell

Edmond *is put in his new cell. His cellmate is a large, black*
Prisoner. **Edmond** *sits on his new bunk in silence awhile.*

Edmond You know, you know, you know, you know we
can't distinguish between *anxiety* and *fear*. Do you know what
I mean? I don't mean fear. I mean, I *do* mean 'fear', I, I don't
mean *anxiety*. (*Pause.*)
We . . . when we *fear* things I think that we *wish* for them.
(*Pause.*) *Death*. Or 'burglars'. (*Pause.*) Don't you think? We
mean we *wish* they would come. Every fear hides a wish.
Don't you think?

Pause.

I always knew that I would end up here. (*Pause.*)
(*To himself.*) Every fear hides a wish.
I think I'm going to like it here.

Prisoner You do?

Edmond Yes, I do. Do you know why? It's simple. That's
why I think that I am. You know, I always thought that *white*
people should be in prison. I know it's the black race we keep
there. But I thought *we* should be there. You know why?

Prisoner Why?

Edmond To be with black people. (*Pause.*) Does that sound
too *simple* to you? (*Pause.*)

Prisoner No.

Edmond Because we're *lonely*. (*Pause.*)
But what I *know* . . . (*Pause.*) What I *know* I think that all this
fear, this fucking *fear* we feel must hide a wish. 'Cause I don't
feel it since I'm here. I *don't*. I think the first time in my life.
(*Pause.*) In my whole adult life I don't feel fearful since I
came in here.
I think we are like birds. I think that humans are like birds.
We suspect when there's going to be an *earthquake*. Birds

know. They leave three days earlier. Something in their soul responds.

Prisoner The birds leave when there's going to be an earthquake?

Edmond Yes. And I think, in our soul, *we*, *we* feel, we sense there is going to be . . .

Prisoner . . . Uh-huh . . .

Edmond . . . a cataclysm. But we cannot flee. We're fearful. All the time. Because we can't trust what we know. That ringing. (*Pause.*)
I think we feel. Something tells us, 'Get *out* of here.' (*Pause.*)
White people feel that. Do you feel that? (*Pause.*) Well.
But I don't feel it since I'm here. (*Pause.*) I don't feel it since I'm here. I think I've settled. So, so, so I must be somewhere safe. Isn't that funny?

Prisoner No.

Edmond You think it's not?

Prisoner Yes.

Edmond Thank you.

Prisoner Thass alright.

Edmond Huh. (*Pause.*)

Prisoner You want a cigarette?

Edmond No, thank you. Not just now.

Prisoner Thass alright.

Edmond Maybe later.

Prisoner Sure. Now you know what?

Edmond What?

Prisoner I think you should just get on my body.

Edmond I, yes. What do you mean?

Prisoner You should get on my body now.

Edmond I don't know what that means.

Prisoner It means to suck my dick. (*Pause.*) Now don't you want to do that?

Edmond No.

Prisoner Well, you jes' do it anyway.

Edmond You're joking.

Prisoner Not at all.

Edmond I don't think I could do that.

Prisoner Well, you going to try or you going to die. Les' get this out the way. (*Pause.*)
I'm not going to repeat myself.

Edmond I'll scream.

Prisoner You *scream*, and you offend me. You are going to die. Look at me now and say I'm foolin'. (*Pause.*)

Edmond I . . . I . . . I . . . I . . . I can't, I can't do, I . . . I . . .

Prisoner The mother*fuck* you can't. *Right* now, missy.

The **Prisoner** *slaps* **Edmond** *viciously several times.*

Prisoner *Right* now, Jim. An' you bes' be nice.

Scene 21

The Chaplain

Edmond *is sitting across from the* **Prison Chaplain**.

Chaplain You don't have to talk.

Edmond I don't want to talk. (*Pause.*)

Chaplain Are you getting accustomed to life here?

Edmond Do you know what happened to me?

Chaplain No. (*Pause.*)

Edmond I was sodomized.

Chaplain Did you report it?

Edmond Yes.

Chaplain What did they say?

Edmond 'That happens.' (*Pause.*)

Chaplain I'm sorry it happened to you. (*Pause.*)

Edmond Thank you.

Chaplain (*pause*) Are you lonely?

Edmond Yes. (*Pause.*) Yes. (*Pause.*) I feel so *alone* . . .

Chaplain Shhhh . . .

Edmond I'm so *empty* . . .

Chaplain Maybe you are ready to be *filled*.

Edmond That's *bullshit*, that's *bullshit*. That's pious *bullshit*.

Chaplain Is it?

Edmond Yes.

Chaplain That you are ready to be filled? Is it impossible?

Edmond Yes. Yes. I don't know what's impossible.

Chaplain Nothing is impossible.

Edmond Oh. Nothing is impossible. Not to 'God', is that what you're saying?

Chaplain Yes.

Edmond Well, then, you're full of *shit*. You understand that. If nothing's impossible to God, then let him let me walk *out* of here and be *free*. Let him cause a new *day*. In a perfect land full of *life*. And air. Where people are *kind* to each other, and there's *work* to do. Where we grow up in *love*, and in security we're *wanted*. (*Pause.*)
Let him do that.
Let him.
Tell him to do that. (*Pause.*) You *ass*hole – if nothing's impossible . . . I think *that* must be *easy* . . . Not: 'Let me *fly*,' or, 'If there is a God make him to make the *sun* come out at

night.' Go on. Please. Please. Please. I'm *begging* you. If you're so smart. Let him do that: Let him do that. (*Pause.*) Please. (*Pause.*) Please. I'm begging you.

Chaplain Are you sorry that you killed that girl?

Pause.

Edmond?

Edmond Yes. (*Pause.*)

Chaplain Are you sorry that you killed that girl?

Edmond I'm sorry about everything.

Chaplain But are you sorry that you killed? (*Pause.*)

Edmond Yes. (*Pause.*) Yes, I am. (*Pause.*) Yes.

Chaplain Why did you kill that girl?

Edmond I . . . (*Pause.*) I . . . (*Pause.*) *I don't* . . . *I* . . . *I don't* . . . (*Pause.*) I . . . (*Pause.*) I don't . . . (*Pause.*) I don't . . . (*Pause.*) I don't think . . . (*Pause.*) I . . . (*Pause.*)

The **Chaplain** *helps* **Edmond** *up and leads him to the door.*

Scene 22

Alone in the Cell

Edmond, *alone in his cell, writes:*

Edmond Dear Mrs Brown. You don't remember me. Perhaps you do. Do you remember Eddie Burke who lived on Euclid? Maybe you do. I took Debbie to the prom. I know that she never found me attractive, and I think, perhaps she was coerced in some way to go with me – though I can't think in what way. It also strikes me as I write that maybe she went of her own free will and I found it important to *think* that she went unwillingly. (*Pause.*) I don't think, however, this is true. (*Pause.*) She was a lovely girl. I'm sure if you remember me you will recall how taken I was with her then.

A **Guard** *enters* **Edmond**'s *cell.*

Guard You have a visitor.

Edmond Please tell them that I'm ill.

Guard *exits.* **Edmond** *gets up. Stretches. Goes to the window. Looks out.*

Edmond (*to himself*) What a day! (*He goes back to his table. Sits down. Yawns. Picks up the paper.*)

Scene 23

In the Prison Cell

Edmond *and the* **Prisoner** *are each lying on their bunks.*

Edmond You can't control what you make of your life.

Prisoner Now, thass for *damn* sure.

Edmond There is a destiny that shapes our ends . . .

Prisoner . . . Uh-huh . . .

Edmond Rough-hew them how we may.

Prisoner How *e'er* we motherfucking may.

Edmond And that's the truth.

Prisoner You *know* that is the truth.

Edmond . . . And people say it's *heredity*, or it's environment . . . but, but I think it's something else.

Prisoner What you think that it is?

Edmond I think it's something *beyond* that.

Prisoner Uh-huh . . .

Edmond *Beyond* those things that we can know. (*Pause.*) I think maybe in dreams we see what it is. (*Pause.*) What do you think? (*Pause.*)

Prisoner I don't know.

Edmond I don't think we *can* know. I think that if we *knew* it, we'd be dead.

Prisoner We would be *God*.

Edmond We would be God. That's absolutely right.

Prisoner Or, or some *genius*.

Edmond No, I don't think even *genius* could know what it is.

Prisoner No, some great *genius*, (*Pause.*) or some *philosopher* . . .

Edmond I don't think even a *genius* can see what we are.

Prisoner You don't . . . *think* that . . . (*Pause.*)

Edmond I think that we can't perceive it.

Prisoner Well, *something's* going on, I'll tell you *that*. I'm saying, *somewhere some* poor sucker knows what's happening.

Edmond Do you think?

Prisoner *Shit* yes. Some whacked-out sucker. Somewhere. In the Ozarks? (*Pause.*) *Shit* yes. Some guy. (*Pause.*) Some *inbred* sucker, walks around all day . . .

Pause.

Edmond You think?

Prisoner Yeah. Maybe not *him* . . . but someone. (*Pause.*) Some fuck locked up, he's got time for reflection . . .

Pause.

Or some fuckin' . . . *I* don't know, some *kid*, who's just been *born*. (*Pause.*)

Edmond Some kid that's just been born . . .

Prisoner Yes. And you know, he's got no precon*ceptions* . . .

Edmond Yes.

Prisoner All he's got . . .

Edmond . . . That's absolutely right . . .

Prisoner *Huh?* . . .

Edmond Yes.

Prisoner Is . . .

Edmond Maybe it's *memory* . . .

Prisoner That's what I'm *saying*. That it just may *be* . . .

Edmond It could be.

Prisoner Or . . .

Edmond . . . or some . . .

Prisoner . . . some . . .

Edmond . . . *knowledge* . . .

Prisoner . . . some . . .

Edmond . . . some *intuition* . . .

Prisoner Yes.

Edmond I don't *even* mean 'intuition' . . . Something . . . something . . .

Prisoner Or some *animal* . . .

Edmond Why not? . . .

Prisoner That all the time we're saying we'll wait for the men from *space*, maybe they're *here* . . .

Edmond . . . Maybe they are . . .

Prisoner . . . Maybe they're *animals* . . .

Edmond Yes.

Prisoner That were *left* here . . .

Edmond *Aeons* ago.

Prisoner *Long* ago . . .

Edmond . . . and have *bred* here . . .

Prisoner Or maybe *we're* the animals . . .

Edmond . . . Maybe we are . . .

Prisoner *You* know, how they, *they* are supreme on their . . .

Edmond . . . Yes.

Prisoner On their *native* world . . .

Edmond But when you put them here.

Prisoner *We* say they're only *dogs*, or *animals*, and *scorn* them . . .

Edmond . . . Yes.

Prisoner We scorn them in our fear. But . . . don't you think? . . .

Edmond . . . It very well could be . . .

Prisoner But on their native *world* . . .

Edmond . . . Uh-huh . . .

Prisoner . . . they are *supreme* . . .

Edmond I think that's very . . .

Prisoner And what *we* have done is to disgrace ourselves.

Edmond We have.

Prisoner Because we did not treat them with respeck.

Edmond (*pause*) Maybe *we* were the animals.

Prisoner Well, thass what I'm saying.

Edmond Maybe they're here to watch over us. Maybe that's why they're here. Or to observe us. Maybe we're here to be punished.

Pause.

Do you think there's a Hell?

Prisoner I don't know. (*Pause.*)

Edmond Do you think that we are there?

Prisoner I don't know, man. (*Pause.*)

Edmond Do you think that we go somewhere when we die?

Prisoner I don't know, man. I *like* to think so.

Edmond I would, too.

Prisoner I sure would like to think so. (*Pause.*)

Edmond Perhaps it's Heaven.

Prisoner (*pause*) I don't know.

Edmond I don't know either but perhaps it is. (*Pause.*)

Prisoner I would like to think so.

Edmond I would, too. (*Pause.*)
Good night. (*Pause.*)

Prisoner Good night.

Edmond *gets up, goes over and exchanges a goodnight kiss with the* **Prisoner**. *He then returns to his bed and lies down.*